CONSTANT COMPANION

"Caution, read Ami Loper's book *Constant Companion* at your own risk. It may leave a permanent mark. With the devotion of a passionate disciple, the competence of a veteran teacher, and the skill of an experienced writer, she invites and inspires us to walk a 'practical path to real interaction with God.' Within its pages, she reveals a thoroughly biblical but deeply personal expression of intimate pursuit that moves the reader's heart to awaken with longing for its Creator. It's a longing that refuses to settle for theology alone and can only be satisfied in moment-by-moment relationship with Him. And if ignited, that desire will shape the rest of your life in both the here and now as well as the forever after."

RANDY BOLDT
Pastor and Author

"Ami Loper is a delightful and gifted woman of God, a dedicated lover and follower of Jesus, a devoted wife and mother, and the youngest-looking grandmother on the planet. For the last twenty-five years, it has been my blessing to have had the privilege of watching her not only become a gifted teacher and speaker but, through her in-depth study of God's Word, a gifted author whose writing opens the heart of the Father to every reader, bringing the Holy Spirit's wrap-around Presence, and His love to minister to both the minds and hearts of her readers. I personally endorse Ami and her book, which is a great read, and an ideal book for personal and spiritual growth and group studies."

JOAN CAVANAUGH BIGGS
Pastor and Author of *More of Jesus, Less of Me*

"*Constant Companion* is an invitation to discover the close and intimate relationship that God wants to have with you! God called Abraham and Moses His friends. The Lord said of Enoch, Noah, Abraham, and Isaac that they walked with Him. *Constant Companion* is a treasure of insights that I recommend you take the time to deep dive into. Much of what Ami shares can become deep wells to the person who has ears to hear, eyes to see, and the heart to understand."

PETE NGAI
Pastor, Hand of Mercy Christian Fellowship

"Ami Loper takes us on a journey with a Divine destination in *Constant Companion*. The invitation is clear, and God's voice is unmistakable as Ami walks us through His Word to discover how much He wants to draw each of us close to Himself. From personal stories, deep insight, and practical application, Ami draws from a deep well of her own experience to escort us in the thrill and life purpose of knowing Jesus as our constant Companion. You won't be disappointed when you open this treasure book for yourself."

SUE BOLDT
Author and Speaker

"Ami reminds us that more than forgiveness, miracles, or breakthroughs, the greatest gift we've been given through the finished work of Jesus is companionship with God Himself. If you're longing to experience the love of the Father and walk in greater intimacy with your Creator, this book is for you."

LAUREN GASKILL
Author, Speaker, and Founder of She Found Joy

"*Constant Companion* is a compelling invitation to experience a deep and personal relationship with the Good Shepherd. In her new book, Ami Loper teaches the reader how to hear and recognize the voice of the Lord while learning to develop an on-going conversation with Him. With sound biblical principles and relevant personal insights, Ami offers practical steps to help the reader move past the obstacles that rob us all from knowing our Savior at the level He desires us know Him."

DR. RICHARD CASTEEL, PASTOR

"I like this book! No, wait, I love this book! Why you ask? Because it is a thorough manual in developing a relationship with our Father in Heaven. It instructs with practical application of becoming more intimate with the Lord Jesus. It emphasizes our relationship with Holy Spirit as a 'growing' relationship. If you have ever doubted that God wants to 'hang out' with you, then you need to read this book. I personally have a renewed desire to grow more intimate with the Lord every day because Ami has challenged me by her words of inspiration with practical application. I have known Ami and her husband, Tim, for several years, and they are the real deal—real people who really love Jesus and love others. I know you will be blessed as you read every page of her latest literary accomplishment, *Constant Companion: Your Path to Real Interaction with God.*"

BUDD RODGERS
Managing Editor, *Fullness Magazine* Online
Fort Worth, Texas

"If you want to take your relationship with God to the next level, then you've got to read this timely book from Ami! In a world where culture is constantly shifting, Ami gently reminds us that our heavenly Father is constant! In her book, she leads us practically to the heart of the Father Who longs to love us and spend time with us. As you read through it, get ready to experience a divine and deeper connection with the One Who created you."

COURTNAYE RICHARD
Blogger, Author, Speaker & Mentor
Founder of Inside Out with Courtnaye
Inside Out Media Group, LLC

"*Constant Companion* is an invitation to come home to God. The author speaks from her heart while providing a theological masterpiece on the relationship between God and humanity. I met Ami Loper when she was a little girl, which afforded me a firsthand view of her life, including her incredible marriage bond with Tim. She is the perfect author for this work because of her beautifully authentic relationship with Christ. Ami walks with God in her mountaintop experiences and her darkest of nights, earning her the relational equity needed to write such a compelling book. The book captivates you as Ami moves her readers beyond the initial invitation to a powerful introduction to her constant Companion."

DR. MARION INGEGNERI, M.A. | THD (H.C.)

CONSTANT COMPANION

YOUR PRACTICAL PATH
TO REAL INTERACTION WITH GOD

AMI LOPER

AMBASSADOR INTERNATIONAL
GREENVILLE, SOUTH CAROLINA & BELFAST, NORTHERN IRELAND
www.ambassador-international.com

CONSTANT COMPANION

Your Practical Path to Real Interaction with God
©2024 by Ami Loper
All rights reserved

ISBN: 978-1-64960-591-7, hardcover
ISBN: 978-1-64960-419-4, paperback
eISBN: 978-1-64960-467-5
Library of Congress Control Number: 2024930089

Cover Design by Hannah Linder Designs
Interior Typesetting by Dentelle Design
Edited by Valerie Coffman

No part of this publication may be reproduced, distributed, or transmitted in any form or by any means, including photocopying, recording, or other electronic or mechanical methods, without the prior written permission of the publisher, except in the case of brief quotations embodied in critical reviews and certain other noncommercial uses permitted by copyright law. For permission requests, contact the publisher using the information below.

Unless otherwise indicated, all Scriptural quotations are taken from the HOLY BIBLE, ENGLISH STANDARD VERSION, ESV. Copyright © 2008 by Crossway, a publishing ministry of Good News Publishers. All rights reserved.

Scripture marked NIV taken from the *NIV Study Bible*, Kenneth L. Barker, General Editor. Grand Rapids, Michigan: Zondervan, 2002.

Ambassador International titles may be purchased in bulk for education, business, fundraising, or sales promotional use. For information, please email sales@emeraldhouse.com.

AMBASSADOR INTERNATIONAL
Emerald House
411 University Ridge, Suite B14
Greenville, SC 29601
United States
www.ambassador-international.com

AMBASSADOR BOOKS
The Mount
2 Woodstock Link
Belfast, BT6 8DD
Northern Ireland, United Kingdom
www.ambassadormedia.co.uk

The colophon is a trademark of Ambassador, a Christian publishing company.

To the One Who wooed relentlessly,

Use this humble offering to woo another.

TABLE OF CONTENTS

PART 1 15
OUR NEED, GOD'S ANSWER

CHAPTER 1
THE COMMON HUNGER   17

CHAPTER 2
GOD'S DESIRE   25

CHAPTER 3
JESUS: THE WAY BACK TO THE GARDEN   35

CHAPTER 4
DEEP CALLS TO DEEP   45

PART 2 53
WHY GO TO THE TROUBLE?

CHAPTER 5
A STRENGTH LIKE NO OTHER   55

CHAPTER 6
TRANSFORMATIVE BENEFITS   63

CHAPTER 7
BEING KNOWN 71

CHAPTER 8
A FRUIT-FILLED LIFE 79

PART 3 85
CHALLENGES TO CONQUER

CHAPTER 9
FEELING UNWORTHY 87

CHAPTER 10
FEELING UNWILLING 99

CHAPTER 11
DISTRACTIONS 113

CHAPTER 12
PREPARE YOUR HEART 121

PART 4 131
A PRACTICAL PATH

CHAPTER 13
MILE MARKERS ON YOUR PATH 133

CHAPTER 14
HOW COMPANIONSHIP IS ATTAINED 139

CHAPTER 15
TROUBLESHOOTING SILENCE 153

CHAPTER 16
WELCOMING AND ABIDING
IN THE PRESENCE   161

BIBLIOGRAPHY   169
ABOUT THE AUTHOR   171

PART 1
OUR NEED, GOD'S ANSWER

CHAPTER 1
THE COMMON HUNGER

ALL OF HUMANITY HAS A common hunger. In a word, it is the desire for "home"—perhaps not the home you are familiar with, perhaps not with all the connotative ideas you have come to associate with the word "home." But surely, if home is to be what it ideally should be, it would be a place where you are known inside and out—all your faults, idiosyncrasies, uniqueness, and beauty—and loved with a love so complete and total that it has the power to heal your pains and renew your mind.

All of us desire to be known and loved. Whether you are old or young, male or female, rich or poor, your heart is searching for an abode with your Creator: a place of companionship, a place of knowing faithful love. We all want reassurance that the love we crave is a love we can find—or that will find us.

GOD GETS THE KEY TO OUR SACREDNESS

You are a sacred creation. The hands of God formed you. Your precious, God-given beauty was meant to be shared. Your heart longs for someone who will see and recognize your exquisite uniqueness. We all want someone to see the "real" us. It's in that comfort of being known and loved that we find the truest sense of home.

It is most natural but also most erroneous to believe that we will find home in other people. When we bravely extend an invitation—holding the key out for someone to gain entry to our hearts—we do so in the hope that they will enter in and see us, know us, and respond to that intimate knowledge with love.

But this is where we have gotten our understanding of "home" turned around. Ideally, we wouldn't look to the people around us first to provide that sense of comfortable ease, fitting in, and being unconditionally loved. Ideally, we would first look into the eyes of our loving Creator and see His love as our haven. He is the only One Who knows us completely, loves us utterly, and knows exactly the longings of our hearts—the heart He designed to beat within us. He is the Match for every searching heart, the Place where our hearts find home.

Instead, fallen human beings expect to find perfect homes with other fallen humans—humans who, no matter how wonderful, can never love us perfectly. Worse, they sometimes tramp through our lives, often leaving brokenness in their wake.

Because the ideal of having our Creator as our first understanding of acceptance and inclusion is rarely, if ever, met, we have experienced life in a backward fashion. Instead of God's approval and love being the backdrop of every other interaction, our view of Him has been distorted by the lens of other loves that came first. We see Him through our wounds instead of seeing our wounds through His love.

If we had beheld His love as our first glimpse of home, we would have seen our identity reflected in His eyes. We would have known who we were by the light and joy shining on His face as He fashioned us in His image and intended us to be His glory-bearers in the world (John 17:22). Our confidence would not hinge on the opinions of broken people but on the established truth that we were imagined in the heart of love, created with wisdom and intention, and set in this world for a purpose.

Instead, we tend to see the eyes of love only after we have adopted the lenses of brokenness. We see God fractured into fragments we have collected along the way, a caricature of reality, grossly misshapen and distorted. We assume He is as temperamental, angry, unreliable, and careless with us as the humans we have trusted have been. And having tried other loves that have failed, injured, or disregarded us, we wonder if anyone will love us, in spite of the damage done. Is there anyone who won't look away in disgust and disappointment but will offer a healing balm?

We feel compelled to fill our hearts and lives hoping to soothe the aching loneliness inside. We have tried inviting people in, but they let us down and caused us pain. We have tried food, material possessions, and exciting experiences; but they either disappointed us or helped for a short time and then left us needing the next dose. We have spent time and money to ease the ache; and at first, we thought we had succeeded. It seemed like we were relieved of the loneliness. But when we got quiet, loneliness returned like a restless resident in our hearts. We can drown out the emptiness for a while, but it will never leave.

HOMELESSNESS

Some time ago, as my husband, Tim, and I joined our church on a homeless outreach, I met a man clad in a cowboy hat, a leather vest, and boots. His befuddled speech flowed out in confused and jumbled stories of loss and disorientation. He had lost his horse and saddle and had his guns taken away. We tried to ascertain his name, but the most he would offer was, "Cowboy."

The more we chatted, the clearer his thoughts became. I learned that this dear man had been all over our nation but could never regain the place he knew in his heart he should be: home. His literal home had been a ranch. But his strongest sensation of home had been on the back of his horse (whom he called his friend) with his other "friends"—his pair of colt rifles. Though he looked the part of a rancher, he was most profoundly homeless.

Cowboy broke my heart that day, but I know God's heart breaks for everyone who is homeless—not just those who have lost their physical houses but also those who have resigned themselves to never knowing the companionship for which we were created.

Like Cowboy, we can look the part—like we have it together, like we belong—and yet be completely lost. There is something for which we are longing beyond a literal house that transcends a sense of comfort that our life's accessories can bring. We long for the abode of belonging that comes from beyond ourselves or anything we can obtain. And even if we know there is something we long for outside ourselves, we can still be utterly without the means of reaching it.

Our hearts will be homeless until our hearts dwell in the One Who promises to be our constant Companion—never leaving, never forsaking. In Jesus Christ, we find those things we have longed for: the sense of being known, the identity, the love we hope to realize in life. We thought we could find it elsewhere—we could practically feel it with our fingertips—yet we were never able to belong until He made it possible.

As C.S. Lewis states, "If I find in myself a desire which no experience in this world can satisfy, the most probable explanation is that I was made for another world. If none of my earthly pleasures satisfy it, that does not prove that the Universe is a fraud. Probably earthly pleasures were never meant to satisfy it, but only to arouse it, to suggest the real thing."[1]

HAPPILY EVER AFTER

It was a dream deep inside of me from my earliest memories, the desire to meet that special someone and marry—the hope of joy, completeness, and a home, where dreams come true. The concept seems to haunt our hearts with

---

[1] C.S.Lewis, *Mere Christianity* (Westwood, New Jersey: Barbour and Company, Inc., 1943), 115.

its promise of ultimate companionship. It tantalizes us with a hope we cannot deny and do not want to live without: the belief that all will be right with the world following one epic day. The great struggle to find love will have ended, and we will be enveloped in a mysterious, enchanting cloud. Bliss will carry us up into the ecstasies of endless joy. The curtain falls. "The End" is written. There is no need to tell any more of that story. We all know what follows. It's the most thrilling phrase ever imagined by my fellow imaginers: "and they lived happily ever after."

The expectation of a "happily ever after" is not even confined to matters of the heart. Yes, romances are an obvious one; but our ideals of success, our waiting on God's promises to us, our dreams and expectations of family, and our visions of what our "somedays" will hold can all live as dreams with expectations of happy endings and complete fulfillment.

But then, it happens. Reality blows away our blissful clouds and breaks the spell. We wake up to find disturbing unhappiness encroaching on our "happily ever after." We find cloud nine makes for an unstable dwelling place. Why didn't anyone tell us you can't live on clouds? You fall right through them like the rest of the sky! And as gravity kicks in and you are hurtling to earth at a nauseating speed, you begin to question why you are falling. *Why does everyone else seem to get away with living on clouds? Is it my fault I'm falling? What is wrong with me that I'm experiencing pain? What happened to my "happily ever after"?*

Hopefully, you have realized by now that you are not alone. Reality strikes everyone. Bumps, pains, and even tragedies come to call on every one of us. But still, the question remains: why would we be given such a desire for love and belonging if it were impossible to achieve? Surely, such a core belief, a universal hope, has a more powerful driving force behind it than fairytale writers. Such a basic human desire must have a purpose.

And indeed, it does. I believe the desire for a happy ending represents the human condition. It's a need for companionship and home. It's the need to be known completely and still loved unconditionally.

UNMET NEEDS

Maybe you don't recognize this need in yourself. Perhaps, for you, this need was met early in life. But for whatever reason, I—and many others like me—feel I do not belong and thus undertake early and often the search for someplace to fit in. And even if the desire to belong was met early in your life, as a child of your loving Heavenly Father, you still need to find your home in Him.

No matter how accepting your family of origin was, they cannot completely meet such an overwhelming need. They were not created for that purpose. Each of us has a gravitational pull, drawing us toward what can make us whole—a pull to the constant Companion Who will never disappoint or leave you because you do not measure up. That pull is a mercy of God, drawing us to Him. Jesus is saying to you, "Behold, I stand at the door and knock. If anyone hears my voice and opens the door, I will come in to him and eat with him, and he with me" (Rev. 3:20).

And yet, unlike inanimate objects, we have the ability and tendency to deny the pull and seek less-fulfilling sources that entice us with empty pledges of wholeness. We seek the mirage of popularity and friendship which has disappointed time after time. We give ourselves over to faulty and incomplete forms of love which seem to have the answers for our lonely souls. We seek fulfillment in money, prestige, beauty, academia, alcohol, or drugs.

THE LONGING FULFILLED

A God-given longing must have a God-given fulfillment. No human can satisfy this hunger. No human is perfect enough. For the perfect "happily ever after" of belonging, we need a perfect Partner.

God has given us this desire in our hearts; and though we run to others, He is always waiting there to show us He is the only truly qualified Answer for the need. The loss of His companionship at the Fall in the Garden of Eden is what has caused the hunger, and He is the only One Who fills it. He formed us to long for a grand romance. And believe me, this romance is far greater than you ever imagined.

Like many other young girls, I was always on the lookout for my own knight in shining armor to come riding on his white steed and take me away, heal the pain of rejection that had so marked me, and breathe love into my lonely soul, so I would come into full bloom. Little did I know, my true Prince *was* pursuing me, and all I had to do was open my spiritual eyes to see Him. He had planned our love story since before I was born, and He longed to be my unfailing Companion and make His home in the secret place of my heart.

But at the time, He seemed so distant, like Someone I had seen only misty images of but could never quite make out. And though I had given my heart to Him, I never imagined He desired to be closer and more real to me than any human being could possibly be. I never realized His longing for me was stronger than my desire to be known. I never realized He was the Source and the Fulfillment of my dreams of love and acceptance. He spent years incessantly cultivating those dreams until they blossomed—first into friendly acquaintance, then into love, and finally into constant companionship.

All my life, I was waiting for a knight in shining armor to ride to me on his white steed. All my life, I knew he would come and rescue me. All my life, I felt he was just around the corner. But I was wrong. My true Hero was not on His way—He was right there beside me, waiting for me to turn and see that He was already there and had been all my life.

THE SNAG IN OUR HAPPILY EVER AFTER WITH GOD

The initial falling in love with our Savior, the One Who has finally made us feel loved and wanted, can help us feel the sense of home we have always longed for. But we need to remove those old mindsets that have us stuck seeing God through faulty lenses. Unless we become equipped to have a relationship with our Creator, the joy of our salvation may be short-lived. We may find ourselves feeling just as much an outsider as we did before. Instead of finding a constant Companion, we have found salvation from a God Who is reaching for us in love while we inadvertently keep Him at arm's length and only catch brief glimpses of His love.

That is the ultimate loneliness—a one-sided relationship. A house can be the loneliest place on earth when the occupants are silent with one another. But that is what many of us have settled for in our relationship with God. We hear others finding hope and joy and direction from a God we feel is so distant.

It is in this void of doubt that the enemy gets in our heads and replays the tapes of rejection, leading us to wonder if God really wants a relationship with us or if He plays favorites with His children. This book was written to fill the void with truth from the Word of God and applied wisdom so that we, too, can know the voice of our constant Companion.

"O God, you are my God; earnestly I seek you; my soul thirsts for you; my flesh faints for you, as in a dry and weary land where there is no water."

Psalm 63:1

CHAPTER 2
GOD'S DESIRE

THIS CONCEPT THAT WE CAN be companions of the God Who created Heaven and earth will stir some questions. Questions are a good thing! It's only by tackling tough questions and settling the conclusions in our hearts that we can build on a solid foundation.

The first question we need to settle will decide whether we continue to pursue companionship or relinquish it as a pipe dream. Does God actually want an intimate relationship with each individual He formed from the dust of the earth, including very messy me? It seems strange to think of the vastness of God longing for the smallness of an individual human being. It may even seem the epitome of conceit on our part to think that the infinite God would want a relationship with finite humans.

Without an answer to this question, there's no purpose in pursuing intimacy. After all, there is no point of pursuing a relationship with Someone Who does not desire to reciprocate. Until we settle this question firmly, we can only speak hypothetically about what such a relationship would look like. Until we know for certain, the doubting question of whether God wants intimacy will only serve to cripple our faith and disable our hope. The road to intimacy with God is arduous; it is not for the faint of heart, nor for those who have not settled this question in their hearts. The enemy will come against this; it is what he fears most. He will try to dissuade you by any means and try to convince you that God is not interested in this type of relationship with you.

It is only as we are firmly established in this truth that we will be able to move forward in our pursuit of such a relationship. Yet as we step back and honestly evaluate the Word of God as a whole, we will discover the answer. Does God want intimacy? It is an astoundingly emphatic yes!

WHY AM I LIKE THIS?

Why is there this longing for home and this sense of homelessness without God? How could a loving Father God create us with a hole in our hearts that longs for home, a hole that causes such longings that we seek to fill it even with painful things?

When studying the Word of God—or even when we are studying human nature—it is important to look at original intent. What was God's original intent for humankind? The Garden of Eden illustrates God's original intent, His perfect plan for the people and the world that He created.

In the garden, humans were created in the context of relationship. The relationship between God and Adam and Eve was perfect. There were no flaws, no imperfections, no barriers, and no fears. God and Adam and Eve enjoyed a relationship of peace, devoid of conflict. Not only were humans created in the context of relationship, but they were also created *for* relationship. Just as fish were created to frolic in water, mountain goats were created to attain great heights, and buffalo were created to roam the plains, humankind was created to bask in the daily enjoyment of intimate companionship with the Creator.

God called His created humanity into intimacy as He walked in the garden to converse with His friend, Adam. And following Adam's rebellion, we can practically hear the pain in God's voice as He asks Adam the haunting question, "'Where are you?'" (Gen. 3:9). As the man and the woman are sent from His intimate Presence, we must recognize the Creator lamented the dreadful separation now broken between Himself and His creation. God grieved not only Adam and Eve's loss but also the loss of all humankind at the Fall. Few human beings would again ascend to an intimate relationship with Him.

But since the moment of the Fall, God has never stopped searching us out. He has never stopped His probing question of "Where are you?" He has never stopped loving, pursuing, or longing for us.

As humans joined the Satanic rebellion against God, we damaged our relationship with God. However, the hole in our hearts left gaping and empty from the tearing away of the Fall has become in each of us the homing device searching out the intimacy with God that was lost. The *need* for intimacy with the Creator never left us; it was embedded in our very nature.

After the Fall, we inherited from our ancestors a brokenness that inhibited our ability to meet that vital need for companionship with God. This inherited relational brokenness carries with it two closely related elements: the fear of exposure and the resulting desire to hide. Because of the fear of exposure, we are just like Adam and Eve, creating fig leaf garments for ourselves, figuratively speaking. We still put up our facades and pretend to not be pitifully naked and ashamed behind them.

Fear of exposure results in a desire to hide. No matter how much we cover up, we know the truth about our own wretchedness, and we fear God's response to it. As Adam and Eve hid from God when they heard the sound of Him walking in the Garden, we still hide from Him, somehow imagining if we ignore Him, He will ignore us. We are like little children in plain sight hiding their eyes and thinking it keeps them unseen.

These partnering impulses—the fear of exposure and the desire to hide—are rooted in our fear of rejection. Why are we afraid? Why do we cover up? Why do we run away when the hands of mercy are extended? We fear rejection.

We know if God, our Creator, rejects us, there is nothing left for us. And rebels as we are, we know we rightly deserve rejection. Not only do we know we deserve rejection for being Adam and Eve's rebellious offspring, but most of us have also experienced it throughout our lives. Again and again, we have been rejected for one reason or another. Those faulty relationships rise up as specters from the grave to condemn us to everlasting alienation from God. In our attempts to avoid the condemnation of rejection, we never give God the chance to speak His truth over us. We busy ourselves, hiding to avoid this core fear of rejection. At the same time, we try to find our comfort in Him and keep Him at a safe distance. The longing to share our sacred abode is the means by which our Father beckons us to Him, encouraging us to invite His love to heal us.

Studying the Fall of humankind brings an interesting question. What exactly is the problem with the Fall? Is it that we will die? If that is the worst thing about it—breaking free from a body that, since the Fall, decays and deteriorates with alarming persistence and speed—then I'm not sure that is a severe enough consequence. The most grievous consequence is the loss of companionship. The garden was our place of belonging; with the Fall, we lost our haven for meeting with God and enjoying fellowship with Him.

MOUNT SINAI

Let's shift from the garden to the desert. When we move from the Garden of Eden to Mount Sinai, we have moved from a place of overflowing abundance in relationship to relational barrenness. From the time of the garden until the time of Moses, it appears there were only a few people from each generation with whom God had an intimate relationship. Sometimes, it's unclear who instigated the relationship. Did God single out individuals, or did individuals seek out God? Regardless, it is clear that something changes at the Exodus.

Following the Exodus of the Israelites from Egypt, God calls the entire nation of Israel to come into covenant relationship with Him. At the foot of Mount Sinai, it begins. God tells the people of His intent toward them and prepares them for what will happen in the next few days. In Exodus 19:4-6, the Lord tells Moses to say to the Israelites, "'You yourselves have seen what I did to the Egyptians, and how I bore you on eagles' wings and brought you to myself. Now therefore, if you will indeed obey my voice and keep my covenant, you shall be my treasured possession among all peoples, for all the earth is mine; and you shall be to me a kingdom of priests and a holy nation.'"

Understand what is happening here. God is reminding the Israelites that it was He Who delivered them from Egypt. Now, He wishes to make a covenant with them in which they agree to obey Him, and He declares that He desires that *all* the people be "'a kingdom of priests and a holy nation'" (v. 6). No longer was one man chosen out of an entire generation; an entire nation was chosen from the world.

"So Moses came and called the elders of the people and set before them all these words that the LORD had commanded him. All the people answered together and said, 'All that the LORD has spoken we will do.' And Moses reported the words of the people to the LORD" (Exod. 19:7-8).

Here, we see that the preliminary agreement to come into covenant relationship has been agreed to by the representatives of the people. Next, Moses receives from God the requirements for the people to consecrate themselves in verses nine through fifteen so that they could all come onto Mount Sinai and see Him. But what actually happened when it was time for everyone to ascend Mount Sinai?

> Now when all the people saw the thunder and the flashes of lightning and the sound of the trumpet and the mountain smoking, the people were afraid and trembled, and they stood far off and said to Moses, "You speak to us, and we will listen; but do not let God speak to us, lest we die." Moses said to the people, "Do not fear, for God has come to test you, that the fear of him may be before you, that you may not sin." The people stood far off, while Moses drew near to the thick darkness where God was (Exod. 20:18-21).

In spite of the fact that God had delivered them, expressed His love to them, and chosen them from among all mankind, the Israelites could not conceive of a God Who was their loving Father. Instead, they drew back in fear and refused to approach God or listen to His voice. Their fears and misconceptions of Who God is kept them from companionship with Him. They were bound by the deeply ingrained slave mentality that saw God as a cruel Master and themselves as fearful slaves. They chose comfortable distance instead of vulnerable intimacy. They reverted to Adam's handbook and hid themselves. They begged for a mediator instead of a personal God.

They allowed their comfort level to take precedence over their higher need to have closeness with God. They sacrificed their necessity of intimacy with their Creator to their temporal need to not be disquieted by Someone dramatically greater than themselves. In the same way, we are individually given the opportunity to come into intimate relationship with the Father. We alone decide how close we are willing to come to God.

Priests were chosen from among the people of Israel as intermediaries between God and the people. But this was not God's original intent, as we have seen in this passage. His original intent was that they would all be "a kingdom of priests and a holy nation" (Exod. 19:6).

THE TABERNACLE

Despite the people's disappointing rejection of God's attempt to connect with them at Mount Sinai, God chose to display a beautiful picture of His desire for us. God created the tabernacle system with its rites and rituals so that the ordinary worshipper may come near—and not only that man would be able to draw near to God, but also that God may abide with us. His desire to live among His people would, in a new manner, be fulfilled. "I will dwell among the people of Israel and will be their God" (Exod. 29:45).

The construction of the tabernacle and the designated areas which God instructed the Israelites to build is a dynamic image of aspects of our relationship with Him. Each area of the tabernacle and each of the pieces of furniture in those areas are for our instruction.

When we look at tabernacle worship, we have a fine line to walk. My first caution is this: it is clear that some of us get stuck in different areas of the tabernacle, while others press forward for more of God. Our flesh would love to allow this truth to become a source of pride so that we begin to look at one another and compare to puff ourselves up. That kind of classification of believers is carnal and will only hinder our progress in intimacy with God.

My second caution is this: there is no road map to intimacy. Our human minds are constantly trying to formulize things so that we can have a clear-cut, step-by-step process to ensure success. This is not the way love relationships work. In tabernacle worship, there are many pictures of what we experience along the way, but be careful of making a formula out of what you see. God does not fit into any mold. He wants an individual relationship with you. You cannot base your relationship with Him on anyone else's. That is part of the beauty of how individually He treats each of us. Embrace that beauty; do not try to contain it.

My final caution is that the tabernacle cannot be seen as a linear process. You do not necessarily finish one step and move on to another as you would in a physical tabernacle. Certain aspects are ongoing, lifelong, and progressive. Some aspects may be complete in certain areas in your life, while they have not even begun in others.

As we look at the tabernacle, bear in mind that the system of the Levitical priesthood was an allowance made by God to the Israelites who chose intermediaries instead of direct connection with God. It was not God's original plan. His plan was that all would freely enter; and as New Covenant believers, we know that intermediaries no longer exist between ourselves and God. We are all called to enter into the very Holy of Holies.

In the tabernacle that Moses saw on Mount Sinai and duplicated on earth, there were three progressive areas that the faithful were intended to experience. In the first section, or outer court of the tabernacle, we see the brazen altar—a place of sacrifice for sin, a place of figuratively burning away our flesh, a place of consecrating ourselves to the Lord, and a place of thanksgiving. It is a stunning picture of our salvation and the place where we decide we want more than salvation. We want to give ourselves wholly to God. Within the first section, but accessible only to the priests, was the bronze basin. It was only accessible to priests who were prepared to go deeper into the tabernacle, and it represents New Covenant believers who have devoted themselves to going deeper with the Lord.

The second section of the tabernacle was the Holy Place. Here, we find three pieces of furniture: the golden lampstand, the table for the bread of the Presence, and the golden altar of incense. All these pieces were hidden from the vast majority of Israelites; only the priests, those consecrated and cleansed, were permitted into the Holy Place.

The lampstand was the only light in the Holy Place and represents that the work of this holy area could only be done by the illumination of the Holy Spirit. The table for the bread of the Presence with its twelve loaves represented the entire community of Israel that the priests embodied. Those loaves were refreshed each week to demonstrate the importance of continual dependence on a fresh experience of the Presence of God. And the golden altar of incense, where the smoke and fragrance of incense rose heavenward, was indicative of worship and prayer.

As the priest passed through the Holy Place, he would fill the golden censor with incense from the golden altar. He would then reach that censor past the thick veil that separated the Holy Place from the Holy of Holies and allow the smoke to fill the Holy of Holies, symbolizing the anointing that worship provides that opens the way to the Presence of God. And pressing past the veil that separated God from those who could not yet come by the way of Jesus Christ, the priest stood before the Ark of the Covenant, a picture of the incarnation of Jesus.

This elaborate ritual, only slightly covered here, was the only means the Israelites knew for meeting with God. It was the only place where Heaven and earth intersected that they could experience. And although it is a weak reflection of the New Covenant believer's path, it shows us something profound—we have the choice of how close we will get to God. We alone choose how much we will pursue Him.

Many Christians do not wish to go any further with God than the brazen altar. They are content to spend their lives celebrating the sacrifice of Jesus on the cross and their redemption. They are at ease within the protective walls of the outer court, where nothing more is required of them, and they can fellowship with other believers. They are saved if they have accepted the saving work of Jesus on their behalf. Nothing more is necessary. Oh, but so much more is *possible*.

There will be a determined few that wish to press forward out of the outer courts into the Holy Place to serve God as we see some of the priests of old did. Then there will also be a handful who wish to go all the way to the Presence of God and see His face. They will not be deterred. They have their hearts set on Heaven, and they can see glimpses of it just beyond their reach. These are the believers who respond to the wooing calls of their Savior and press onward to the Holy of Holies.

> *"Who shall ascend the hill of the LORD? And who shall stand in his holy place? He who has clean hands and a pure heart."*
>
> Psalm 24:3-4

CHAPTER 3
JESUS: THE WAY BACK TO THE GARDEN

WHY IS IT THAT ANTS so often seem to choose the most inconvenient spots to make their dwelling places? We have an ant colony under a big shade tree in our backyard right near the prettiest flowers that my grandkids want to pick and sniff. One day, panic struck when I suddenly discovered ants crawling on my grandson's legs, and he was repeatedly bitten. He kept asking why. Why did they want to bite him? He wasn't hurting them.

It is frustratingly impossible to communicate with ants, to tell them you mean them no harm. In fact, the more you try, the more they are likely to think you are attacking them and will fight back! If only I could temporarily become like one of them, I would be able to communicate with them. I could tell them that we mean them no ill will but that they must live in another part of the yard to be safe.

This made me think about the history of humanity and God's attempts to communicate with us. From the beginning of time, He desired connection and communion with mankind. He walked with Adam and Eve in the garden. But when these humans elevated their own reasoning above the wisdom of God, their communication became limited.

Yet God still desired to communicate His will, His love, and His plans to mankind. He founded a system of tabernacle worship to attempt to communicate that He desired people to come into fellowship with Him. Yet often, they only see with a skewed perspective. Instead of seeing all this as God's attempt to reach out to them, they saw a list of do's and don'ts that they thought were a means of perfecting themselves enough to be worthy of God.

Still, God's desire continued; and He sent prophets, His mouthpieces, to communicate His love and passion for the people and His desire that they would see Him as He is—the only true God Who desires fellowship with humankind.

From the garden all the way through the Old Testament, the Father was there communicating His love, demonstrating His desire for communion and shouting out His mercy and compassion and righteousness through the prophets. Like ants hearing a human speaking to them, most of humankind could only hear the voice, but they never perceived what He said. And interwoven in all He said was the promise that He would one day do the unthinkable: become one of us.

And that is precisely what He did. More extraordinary than a human becoming a puny ant, Jesus chose to lay aside His glory and become a man. He came to communicate His love, holiness, and desire for intimacy with humankind. And when He had sufficiently communicated this, He made it possible that we could exchange our moral inadequacy for His holiness and commune with Him as Adam and Eve did. He did this by surrendering His life and becoming the Payment for all our sins.

He did all this with one solitary purpose in mind—a renewed garden, a new home of communion together, a new era in which man and God could meet with one another. His desire from Creation—a desire for an intimate relationship with humankind—is finally possible through His own plan and sacrifice. And all we have to do is accept it by faith.

What an extraordinary God! He chose to lay aside His rights as God in order to meet with us on our lowly level to demonstrate His vast love and then to bring us up to His level. It is truly astonishing and astonishingly true.

From Creation, God knew the Fall would happen, and His remedy for the great separation was already set in motion. Jesus was there all along, though at the time, we did not know Him by name. He was already willing to do the Father's will to ensure that all who called on His name would be reunited in the intimacy that had been lost. He would accomplish it all, and He would do it through a four-fold process that would transform the destiny of planet Earth and every human being. The four distinct steps in this process that transformed us are the incarnation, the crucifixion, the resurrection, and the ascension.

THE INCARNATION

With the incarnation, God was able to speak to humankind firsthand to tell them of His love and of His plan to finally do away with sin so that they might enter freely into His Presence and recapture that Garden of Eden experience of walking with God without the sin barrier.

John 1:14 explains, "And the Word became flesh and dwelt among us, and we have seen his glory, glory as of the only Son from the Father, full of grace and truth." The Lord Jesus came in the tent of flesh and tabernacled among us. He came as a Divine Man to communicate to us the heart of the Father.

He taught a close group of people and made it abundantly clear that they had no means of acquiring Heaven based on their own unattainable perfection or by the goodness of their deeds. He made the need felt, so they were forced to ask the pivotal question, "How then can we be saved?"—a question He answered through His actions on the cross.

He also defended the cause of the poor and oppressed. He defended them by way of example and then left it to His followers to walk the same way, thereby becoming agents of change in the world. Jesus' seemingly simple actions have an interesting implication that runs contrary to the experience of the cultures around it: equality among humankind. By action, He made it clear that access to the Father is not reserved for the rich, the elite, or the professionally religious. It is not dependent on birth, rank, race, or gender. All are invited.

THE CRUCIFIXION

I used to wonder why Jesus did not teach longer. It is obvious in the Scriptures that Jesus went to Jerusalem that last time knowing He would be crucified. Why did He not stay away, so He could spend more time with His disciples? They certainly did not seem ready for worldwide ministry by my human standards, and I personally would love to hear more of what was in my Lord's mind and heart. So why, after only three-and-a-half years of ministry, did He choose to go to Jerusalem and lay down His life?

As I have pondered this, I have felt the Holy Spirit reminding me that the teaching part of Jesus' ministry was not His primary objective in the incarnation. As a teacher myself, I love teaching and always want more of Jesus' words. And although it was vital to speak and demonstrate the heart of God, the incarnation had one primary objective—the crucifixion.

For so long, we have supposed that the problem God was working to solve through the crucifixion was a sin problem. What we really had was an intimacy problem. It was intimacy that was lost; it is intimacy God whispered about to us through the ages; it is intimacy He died to restore. Sin was the agent of separation but is now removed from the equation for those who have accepted the sacrifice of Jesus as their Substitution. Now, the question remains: will you walk in the intimacy that Jesus Christ died to restore to you?

Sin *was* the barrier that kept us from intimacy; but when we limit our problem to sin, many come to the Lord, have their sins forgiven, and think that's the end of the problem. But when we recognize that we actually have an intimacy problem, we are more apt to recognize that taking care of the sin issue enables us to remedy the true problem and pursue relational intimacy.

In John 17:3, Jesus says, "And this is eternal life, that they know you, the only true God, and Jesus Christ whom you have sent." In this statement, Jesus makes it clear that the issue of salvation has less to do with removal of sin and more to do with deeply knowing God. And knowing God is all about restoration of the intimacy lost at the Fall.

The "intimacy problem" was remedied by Jesus becoming our Substitution and visible Example of that separation through the crucifixion and by dealing with our sin barrier on the cross. Before the cross, all humans were members of the line of Adam. We all inherited our father Adam's sin nature and his death sentence. But after the cross, we were given the choice to "opt out" of being considered as part of the line of Adam. New Covenant believers belong to a new line by which we trace our heritage, identity, and destiny.

For our heritage, we are of the line of Abraham through our faith (Rom. 4 and Gal. 3). Because he is the "father of faith," all who have faith in God are his offspring. God has indeed raised up stones as offspring to Abraham (Luke 3:8).

As for our identity, we are of the line of Christ. We are co-heirs with Him, and we are to bear His image in the earth. "As was the man of dust [Adam], so also are those who are of the dust, and as is the man of heaven [Christ], so also are those who are of heaven. Just as we have borne the image of the man of dust, we shall also bear the image of the man of heaven" (1 Cor. 15:48-49).

And we are of the line of Christ with regard to our destiny. As 1 Corinthians 15:20-22 says, "But in fact Christ has been raised from the dead, the firstfruits of those who have fallen asleep. For as by a man [Adam] came death, by a man [Christ] has come also the resurrection of the dead. For as in Adam all die, so also in Christ shall all be made alive."

At the cross, God would do the unthinkable. He would temporarily separate Himself from His precious Son. As Jesus hung on the cross, He took on all the weight and burden of all sin, from the Fall to the end of time. God turned His face from His Son. It is at this moment we hear the echoed, anguished cry that God spoke on the day of the Fall. As God had asked Adam "'Where are you?'" (Gen. 3:9), Jesus now cries out, "'My God, my God, why have you forsaken me?'" (Matt. 27:46).

And now, because of that momentary separation that the Father and Son endured, the veil has been torn asunder, and the Father's creation is encouraged to come boldly before the throne of grace. With our stain of sin removed by the precious blood of Jesus making us blameless in the sight of God, we may commune with God. We may walk with Him in His garden once again. Because of God's redemptive act, intimacy is an open invitation to all who will.

THE RESURRECTION

Although we annually celebrate the resurrection of Jesus from the dead and sing and rejoice over it, many are unaware of the significance of exactly what it means to our spiritual existence that Jesus Christ rose from the dead. Why would Paul write in 1 Corinthians 15:17, "If Christ has not been raised, your faith is futile and you are still in your sins"? By resurrecting Jesus, God showed to the world that He had accepted Jesus' payment for sin.

How do we know that the payment for our sins has been accepted by God? By the resurrection! How do we know that there is life beyond the grave? By the resurrection! How do we know that we will one day rise again? By the resurrection! By the resurrection, we have the assurance that we have been justified by the blood of Jesus, that God has accepted the exchange of the righteous blood of Jesus as the redemptive payment for our lives, and that He has purchased us out of slavery to live in freedom and life. We know that when we die, we will not spend eternity separated from God in some netherworld or in Hell. We will "dwell in the house of the LORD forever" (Psalm 23:6).

By the resurrection, we have the assurance that Jesus is Lord and that the sacrifice on the cross successfully dealt with the barrier of sin. And with the barrier gone, we can now press with confidence into that intimate relationship for which our hearts are longing.

Consider the remarkably prophetic statement of Hosea 6:2. It hints at us from hundreds of years before Jesus' death and resurrection, "After two days he will revive us; on the third day he will raise us up, that we may live before him." This verse speaks of the judgment that had come upon Israel for their idolatry, yet it promises that after judgment, God is in the resurrecting business! Under the New Covenant, He brought all that judgment to bear on Jesus, and we are the beneficiaries. But notice the purpose for which He raised us up: "that we may live before him." His purpose was for us to be brought into relationship.

Jesus was resurrected as the firstfruits of the resurrection of all (1 Cor. 15:20). Now we can all be resurrected—not just when we die in our flesh, but also our spirits can be resurrected *now* out of the death they all experienced at the Fall. Our spirits died at the Fall; yet life is available to them through salvation.

THE ASCENSION

The ascension is yet another way in which the Lord leads us by example. He clearly showed His disciples that there is a pathway open to the Father and that He has gone to prepare that way for us. It is not exclusively a way to Heaven, a way to be with the Father in the sweet by-and-by; it is a way that is now accessible to all who trust in Jesus as their way. It is the way of communion with the Father *now*.

Through the ascension, we are shown the position of Christ. Having opened for us "the new and living way" to the Father (Heb. 10:20), He is now "at the right hand of the throne of the Majesty in heaven" (Heb. 8:1), and we are assured that He is there ever making intercession for us (Heb. 7:25). We see through the eyes of the disciples that Jesus is not mere man but God and Man, and He has taken His rightful place.

By seeing this, we are also assured of our own place. Paul says in Ephesians 2:6 that God "raised us up with [Christ] and seated us with him in the heavenly places in Christ Jesus." Christ's ascension provides us with the assurance that all that He promised us about the life of the members of the new family is indeed ours. We have been disconnected from the line of Adam and grafted into Abraham to become children of God. He has accomplished it all.

THE PURPOSE OF CREATION

The Word of God teaches that the purpose of the entire world from creation onward is to bring glory to God (Psalm 19:1-4). What is it that brings the most glory to God? What is it that brings the blend of perplexed awe and worship from every heavenly being? It is that God loved His own creation enough to die for it (Eph. 1:3-12).

All the effort of pursuit and wooing throughout the Old Testament point to this purpose. When Jesus became flesh, taught, healed, died, rose again, and ascended to the throne, He had one aim: that God would be glorified. God is glorified through the revelation of Who He is—the all-wise, all-loving God. He is the God Who would do anything required to return His creation back to its garden position where work, love, and life were all within the context of intimate relationship.

What we have missed so often in the Church Era is the fact that we do not have to wait for Heaven to begin that life. Jesus came that we might have life to the fullest now on earth. Granted, undying bodies and tearless days wait until we pass beyond the border into Heaven, crossing through the very death the enemy had hoped would be our destruction but has now lost its sting (1 Cor. 15:55-58). But the relationship, the intimacy, the place of "home" and belonging is available now. The veil has been torn, and entrance into the Holy of Holies is available to all. We may with confidence approach the throne. We may walk in the garden with Him once again.

In addition, by rending the veil through His death, Jesus demonstrated that He had completely covered the requirements of the Law, placing His everlasting blood on the mercy seat. All that remains is for us to boldly enter into His Presence and enjoy the intimacy He died to restore (1 Peter 3:18).

Now *we* are the tabernacles of God. His act in the Heavenly Holy of Holies has commissioned us for our mission on earth. For "God . . . does not live in temples made by man" (Acts 17:24). But as believers, we have the Holy Spirit dwelling within us. First Corinthians 6:19 states, "Your body is a temple of the Holy Spirit within you." That word "temple" is *naos* in the Greek; and whereas the Greek word *hieron* refers to an entire temple precinct, *naos* specifies the inner sanctuary, the Holy of Holies. *You* are this Holy of Holies now! *You* are the dwelling place of God. Access to it is entirely within your reach.

CONCLUSION

Now, as New Covenant believers, intimacy is attainable—not for a few, but for all. But this question remains: will we respond to His love pursuit? Will we enter into the relationship that He died to make possible? All Jesus did cannot remedy the longing of God's heart. It was for the purpose of restoring intimate fellowship with mankind that Jesus came. God continues to reach out to all men, not only so that they will be saved and welcomed into His family but also to go further and come to know Him intimately. He longs that He would not only be permitted to enter your heart but that you would press forward to enter His.

The long centuries in which God has set the scene for His love of humanity to be revealed have all converged into the spectacular culmination of the incarnation, crucifixion, resurrection, and ascension of Jesus Christ. Now, we must choose to respond—not just by dealing with the sin barrier but also by going the full distance and finding that place of intimate acceptance.

I was looking deeper into a familiar passage recently, and I found one of my biggest pet peeves—a lousy translation! I'm sure you are all familiar with the verse in Genesis that talks about the Lord God coming to walk in the Garden of Eden in the "cool of the day" (3:8). The word that is translated "cool" here is actually *ruach*, and it means "spirit"—and usually the Spirit of God. In fact, Genesis 3:8 is the only place it is ever translated "cool." Likely, this Scripture should read that God came to walk with Adam and Eve in the "age or era of the Spirit." Indeed, this was an era in which there was no barrier between the Spirit of God and the spirit of man. There was sweet communion.

Now, we may again experience the "Age of the Spirit" in which God walks with us and talks to us as He did in the garden. What an unimaginable thing the God of the universe has done to regain communion with us! He Himself has come and given Himself as the sacrifice to obtain the right for us to have oneness with Him once again.

This is the reason He came: to reunite us with God—to establish Himself as the Way to enter into that reunion, to allow us to experience that garden experience.

> *"For in him all the fullness of God was pleased to dwell,*
> *and through him to reconcile to himself all things,*
> *whether on earth or in heaven, making peace by the blood of his cross."*
>
> Col. 1:19-20

CHAPTER 4
DEEP CALLS TO DEEP

ANYTHING LESS THAN TRUE COMPANIONSHIP with God leaves us feeling on the fringes, close but not close enough. Short of companionship, we will end up feeling as we have often felt before—the last one picked for the team, the third wheel, the odd man out, the one who just cannot figure out how to fit in.

Despite its overuse and popularity (or perhaps because of it), "intimacy" can be a vague term. I have intentionally tried to steer away from it up to this point, using other words such as "companionship." But let me be clear that by using "companionship," I am not implying any kind of casual relationship. In truth, for all the challenges of its overuse and misuse, "intimacy" is the best word to describe the depth of companionship to which I refer. Intimacy is where the deep places in me call out to the deep places in God, and He graciously calls back to me. It is the intimacy seen in Psalm 42 when the hungry, cast-down soul pours out all to God only to realize that God fills his weary soul with assurances of His promises to see him through to the place of restoration and peace.

To get a clear reference point for what I will mean when I refer to "intimacy" or "companionship," let's look at the way the Bible defines it from which we will derive an applicable definition.

THE HEBREW DEFINITION

The Old Testament speaks often of knowing God. Jeremiah 9:23-24a states, "Thus says the LORD: 'Let not the wise man boast in his wisdom, let not the mighty man boast in his might, let not the rich man boast in his riches, but let him who boasts boast in this, that he understands and knows me.'" The Hebrew word translated "knows" in this verse is the word *yada*.

"'To know' God is to have an intimate experiential knowledge of Him."[2] This verse in Jeremiah explains this type of intimate relationship as more important than wisdom, might, or riches; and it alone is worthy of our boasting. No other condition or quality in the world compares to knowing God intimately.

Yada is used throughout the Hebrew Scriptures to express a depth of relationship beyond simply being acquainted with another person. It goes much deeper than knowing about a person, as we will discover. The word *yada* speaks so profoundly of intimacy that it is also the word used in Genesis 4:1: "Adam knew Eve." Here, it is used to indicate the most intimate of human relationships, the sexual relationship between a husband and wife. *Yada* is a knowledge which comes experientially and through closeness and intimacy. *Yada* entails spending time with another person in order to know their heart.

Yada is also the word used when Moses pleads with the Lord to be permitted to "know" Him in Exodus 33:13: "Now therefore, if I have found favor in your sight, please show me now your ways, that I may *know* you in order to find favor in your sight" (emphasis mine).

Let us consider for a moment the context of Moses asking God for this type of relationship. Thus far in Moses' relationship with God, he has experienced Him in profound ways. Moses has learned of his own Hebrew lineage, knew he was called by God to be the deliverer of his people from slavery in Egypt, and attempted to enact this calling by his own power through the murder of

---

[2] W.E. Vine, *Vine's Complete Expository Dictionary of the Old and New Testament Words* (Nashville, Tennessee: Thomas Nelson, Inc.,1996), 131.

an Egyptian (Acts 7:23-25). He has spent forty years tending sheep, climaxing in a conversation with God at a burning bush, where he speaks freely with God, learns God's proper name, and sees God perform signs and wonders, even in Moses' own body. Moses then returned to Egypt, where he allowed himself to be used by God as His mouthpiece before Pharaoh. He has seen God perform remarkable signs throughout the most powerful country on the planet at that time. He has led the Israelites out of Egypt, a feat impossible without the miraculous intervention of God. He led them through the Red Sea and to Mount Sinai. He ascended Mount Sinai and saw the thick darkness surrounding God as God set out the covenant's stipulations. He held tablets of stone upon which God Himself wrote. He even saw the real temple of Heaven, of which the earthly tabernacle was to be a copy.

After all of these amazing interactions with God, working alongside Him, doing His will, and being His instrument in the earth, Moses says, "I want to *yada* You."

If there was ever a man on earth who could qualify as knowing God, it would have been Moses, prior to this request. Yet he wants more. He wants to not just know *about* Him or *work with* Him. He wants intimacy.

THE GREEK DEFINITION

In the New Testament, which is written in Greek, there are several words translated "know." The words *oida* and *eido* mean to know a thing intuitively. These words do not describe intimacy. However, the Greek word *ginosko* is also translated "know" and means to know experientially. It is the word most equivalent to our Hebrew word, *yada*.

Ginosko is the word used when Jesus says, "And this is eternal life, that they know [*ginosko*] you, the only true God, and Jesus Christ whom you have sent" (John 17:3). By this, Jesus is telling us that redemption is more than having our sins forgiven; it is an intimate relationship He came to restore between us and God. If we are going to live out the first and greatest commandment of loving God completely (Matt. 22:36-37), this is the type of experiential intimacy which ought to be the objective of our lives.

As with the Hebrew word *yada*, *ginosko* is also used to indicate the physically intimate relationship between husband and wife (Matt. 1:25)—again, the most intimate relationship between humans.

A WORKING DEFINITION

Because of the clear overlap between the definition of the Greek word *ginosko* and the Hebrew word *yada*, we will treat them as synonyms. Combining these definitions and applying them to our lives and relationship with our Heavenly Father, we arrive at the following definition of intimacy with God: To know God intimately is to be fully acquainted with Him in an ever-increasing, ever-deepening measure, to know Him through all of our senses, to experience Him in His fullness, in His realm of the Spirit, and see Him at work in our human experience. To know God is to have the deep and abiding sense of His loving Presence regardless of where we may be or what we may be doing. To know Him involves a connection of our heart to His, through communication and continual awareness of His Presence. This experience will invariably bring about a change in our hearts as they line up with His heart. By knowing Him, we will enter into the realm of the Spirit where He dwells and then carry that experience into the realm of the natural where others may also experience Him through us.

RELATIONSHIP AND RIGHTEOUSNESS

In the Word of God, we see repeatedly that a love relationship with God and righteousness (right standing with God) are inextricable. To be righteous is to know the Lord intimately. It's no coincidence when the teacher of the

Law comes to Jesus in Matthew 22:34-40 and asks Him what the greatest commandment is (the most important Law to keep) that Jesus answers him not in terms of right and wrong or in terms of how to remain clean according to the Law, but in terms of relationship. He speaks of the need for loving God with all that is within you. If you want righteousness, seek relationship. They go hand in hand.

Conversely, often in the Bible, we see unrighteousness is equated to not having relationship with the Lord. In Job 18:21, we see a parallel between the "unrighteous" and the one who "knows not God." It says, "Surely such are the dwellings of the unrighteous, such is the place of him who knows [*yada*] not God." And we see it in the discussion of Eli's evil, worthless sons who "did not know [*yada*] the LORD" (1 Sam. 2:12).

Jesus calls us into relationship with the Father—intimate relationship. That relationship *is* righteousness.

BEING A SHEEP OF THE GOOD SHEPHERD

In John 10, Jesus spreads out a beautiful picture of relationship with Him. It is the relationship between sheep (us) and Shepherd (Him). On the surface, this is not that complimentary to us, the sheep. Sheep are rather dumb animals, but they have a quality about them that we are to emulate. They listen.

Jesus revealed to the people that He was their Good Shepherd, that He would lay His life down for the sheep. But He didn't stop at laying His life down; He wanted more. He explained that those who are His sheep would know the voice of their Good Shepherd, and they would follow Him.

The result of being with our Shepherd, of developing companionship with Him, is that we know Him and His voice. We can even discern between His voice and the voice of another. Jesus said that His sheep would flee from the voice of strangers.

Sometimes, we get it backward. We listen too much to our own voices or to the voice of an enemy who would drag us away. Is hearing from the Good Shepherd a pipe dream or exclusively for important moments or important people?

Are you a sheep? If you are saved, you are. And if you are a sheep, you should be hearing your Good Shepherd.

KNOWING ABOUT GOD VERSUS KNOWING GOD

As I have already hinted, intimacy must be more than knowing the facts about God. Intimacy involves knowing Him for ourselves. We cannot ride anyone else's coattails into the presence of God. We cannot get there based on what group we are with, what good things we have done, or by how popular we are with the right people. Consider, if you will, Jesus' warning to those who did all the right things and appeared to have a relationship with Him. He says, "'I never knew you; depart from me'" (Matt. 7:23).

People who knew me a long time ago may know about me, but they do not have a relationship with me. People who read things I have written or hear me preach may know personal details about my life. Again, these people can get to know much *about* me without ever developing an intimate relationship with me.

How many of us know about God but do not know God personally, intimately? Maybe, like me, you have been haunted with the image of being someone who prophesied and cast out demons in the name of the Lord, only to have the Lord say, "'I never knew you'" (Matt. 7:22-23).

The truth is, I could read my Bible twenty-four seven and study all kinds of Christian books and end up knowing all *about* God. But that would not mean I know Him. It would only mean I knew certain facts about God. That is not what I want.

But it takes time. It takes attention. It takes energy. Even with human relationships, it's tiring to think about building meaningful companionship. We want to have coffee once or twice with someone and say we know them.

I know my husband because since 1990, we have walked through life—the great times and the heart-wrenching. We have sat and talked for hours, but we have also worked alongside each other. We have played and laughed and fought and cried. I know what makes him happy and energized, and I know what makes him hurt or discouraged. I know him. I have walked with him.

WALKING WITH GOD

I want to walk with God. I want to know Him and His heart. I don't want to sip my tea while I chat about the few issues on *my* mind. I don't want to interview Him like a reporter simply to get answers to the questions I need answered. I have been interviewed before and cannot even remember the interviewer's name! I don't want to have known Him in the past and only keep in touch at holidays or when I'm in trouble. I want more of a relationship than that with my *Abba*, my Father.

I want to walk with my God as Enoch and Noah did. I want to experience His presence every moment of my day. I want Him to make His habitation with me—my heart, His home. I want God to call me His friend. I want to be like Job, who describes his relationship with God as "intimate friendship" (Job 29:4 NIV). I want to be taken into God's confidence like David and Amos (Psalm 25:14, Prov. 3:32, Amos 3:7, Amos 4:13).

I don't want artificial familiarity and uncultivated intimacy. My desire is to know God in an ever-increasing, ever-deepening measure. My deepest desire is to be so intimately acquainted with Him that when we finally meet one another face to face, He and I will not be strangers, no not us! It will be the beautiful next step of a grand romance. We will know one another such that His expression speaks His heart straight to mine. When I am in His arms at last, it will be a familiar intimacy and warmth of at last being *home*.

One of my favorite verses gives a beautiful picture of intimacy with *Abba*. Jeremiah 26:19 says Hezekiah entreated the favor of the Lord. But if you look at the original Hebrew, it literally says Hezekiah "stroked His face" or "patted His cheek." Is there a more intimate picture? Hezekiah was relationally close enough to approach the Almighty God and stroke His face! I picture myself just crawling up into His generous lap and in peace, stillness, and adoration, caressing the face of God. This is my heart's deepest desire and highest aspiration.

We can rest our hopes and aspirations of truly knowing our God on this promise: "You will seek me and find me, when you seek me with all your heart" (Jer. 29:13).

> *"O my dove, in the clefts of the rock, in the crannies of the cliff,*
> *let me see your face, let me hear your voice, for your voice is sweet,*
> *and your face is lovely."*
>
> Song of Songs 2:14

PART 2
WHY GO TO THE TROUBLE?

CHAPTER 5
A STRENGTH LIKE NO OTHER

WHEN YOU FIND YOUR PLACE of belonging in the Lord, certain things are going to begin to change for you. It is inevitable. Closeness with the Lord naturally brings certain benefits. But I would also encourage you that many of the benefits we will discuss will not appear out of thin air. They can be missed if we aren't watching for them, expecting them in faith, and cultivating them when we see their seedling selves begin to emerge in our lives.

When I was a child, I had the incomparable blessing of growing up near all four of my grandparents. It was great, and there was nothing better than going over to their houses and spending the day. I cherish them and the memories they provided.

One result of going over to my mom's parents' house was that after you had been there, everyone knew it. They were smokers. Granddaddy smoked a pleasant-smelling pipe, and Grandmommy smoked cigarettes—a lot of cigarettes. Everything you had been wearing there had to be laundered. The smell even saturated your hair! But it was worth it to spend time in their lives, laughing, playing, and shouting to be heard over the din of whatever ballgame Granddaddy had on.

I was thinking about this the other day when I was pondering the names of God, names like *Yahweh Shalom* (God my Peace), *Yahweh Tsidkenu* (God my Righteousness), and *Yahweh Rophe* (God my Healer). I was thinking about the fact that because I am in a covenant relationship with God, this peace, this righteousness, and this healing are mine. But how exactly do I access them?

That is when the image of my precious grandparents came into view. Proximity makes the difference. The closer I got to my grandparents, the more what was on them got on me. The more I became identifiable with them, the more I had what they had. (Yes, I know that smelling of smoke is not that attractive, but stay with me!)

"So, Lord," I said, "what You are saying is that the closer I get to You, the more of what naturally exudes from You will infiltrate and saturate me!" In fact, God doesn't just *have* peace, righteousness, and healing—God *is* Peace; God *is* Righteousness; God *is* Healing! And because God is all these things, the more time I spend in His presence. And the more intimate I am with Him, the more I will naturally be saturated by all that He offers.

I am just getting over a head cold as I write this. I don't exactly know who gave it to me, but I bet it was someone I love! Most of what I catch is transmitted from those closest to me. Is that not the way? I need a new transmission, a better transmission. I want what God is transmitting. If it is His peace I need, how do I get that? Get closer! I climb up in His lap and rest a while. I give my burdens to Him (1 Peter 5:7) and leave them there to soak in His peace.

What a blessed place to be and what a reassurance to know that once I have spent some time with Him there in His house, I will smell more like Him.

What rubs off on us more and more the closer we get to the Lord are spiritual benefits. They are the side effects of what happens for us when we spend time in His presence. Of course, we are pursuing the Lord for His own sake because we have fallen for Him like we have never fallen for anyone before. Nevertheless, even when we are focusing on the Giver rather than the gifts, these spiritual benefits will show up.

BEING ROOTED

Paul speaks twice of being "rooted." To the Ephesians, he says that he is praying, "So that Christ may dwell in your hearts through faith—that you, being rooted and grounded in love, may have strength to comprehend with all the saints what is the breadth and length and height and depth, and to know the love of Christ that surpasses knowledge, that you may be filled with all the fullness of God" (3:17-19). Note that it is only after we are rooted in the love of God (an intimate awareness of His love) that we will be empowered to grasp just how much Jesus loves us. And even then, Paul says that we will know that this love surpasses our ability to comprehend it! The knowledge of it is too wonderful and too vast for our human minds to conceive; yet by this realization, we will be overflowing with the completeness of God Himself! What a spectacular promise for those who choose to go deeper than the surface-level relationship and become rooted in God.

Again, in Colossians, Paul mentions being "rooted." "Therefore, as you received Christ Jesus the Lord, so walk in him, rooted and built up in him and established in the faith, just as you were taught, abounding in thanksgiving" (2:6-7). Here it is even clearer that Paul refers to something beyond salvation when he refers to being rooted. He describes the process as moving from initial salvation to continuing to live *in* Jesus. Living in Him speaks of an intimate relationship that goes deeper than what many of us have experienced. This deeper relationship leads to a strengthening of our faith and a heart overflowing with gratitude. Like a tree in a storm that has its roots deep in the ground, it will not be blown over in the gale.

"The root of the righteous will never be moved."

Prov. 12:3b

POWER

I don't know about you, but I'm often faced with circumstances that try to steal my peace. A child or grandchild in trouble, a potential disagreement with a friend, a sick parent, a world that seems constantly on the brink of disaster all contrive to rob me of the peace and strength that is mine as a gift from the Lord.

If I know what God says about a situation, I have the power to stand in faith regardless of what trouble may be brewing. But to know God's truth about specific situations for which the Bible is unclear, I must practice the ability to hear from Him and bring my heart into alignment with what He says.

Being able to hear the voice of my Lord fosters trust that gives me the power to stand toe to toe against any opponent and speak God's truth into reality, calling His Kingdom to come into my situation.

In the book of Daniel, we are told that "the people who *know* their God shall stand firm and take action" against the attacks of the mightiest of oppressors (Dan. 11:32, emphasis mine). This type of power is not available to the casual Christian but only to those who have exerted themselves to know the Lord to such a depth that nothing can shake them.

> *"He gives power to the faint, and to him who has no might he increases strength. Even youths shall faint and be weary, and young men shall fall exhausted; but they who wait for the LORD shall renew their strength; they shall mount up with wings like eagles; they shall run and not be weary; they shall walk and not faint."*
>
> Isa. 40:29-31

PEACE

Lately, I have felt like I'm in a whirlwind season. Ever had one of those? It feels like I cannot catch my breath; and I will admit, sometimes my priorities have suffered. But it seems that no matter how fast I run to accomplish tasks so that I can recapture my priorities, it just does not work that way. I only end up breathless and burned out. One of my daily priorities that has suffered a bit of late is my daily time of listening to the Lord's voice. Oh, I have been praying and studying and focusing on Him, but I have been spotty in my commitment to just sit and listen. Consequently, my peace has suffered.

I marvel at the fact that God made this entire world by speaking it into existence. The mighty mountains, the surging seas, the intricate wildlife, and far-reaching heavens all came into being at His command. But you and I are different. His hands held the unformed me, and He breathed Spirit breath into my body. And yet, each and every day, I need new breath, a new opportunity for His Spirit to connect with mine. I cannot breathe just once a day and expect that I can make it on that one breath for the day. I believe God created us with this inability as a sign of our dependence on Him and His presence.

What a pity when I neglect this time. It isn't as though God punishes me for it or gets mad at me. But what peace and blessing I miss out on when I fail to prioritize my intimacy with Him. The gloriousness of allowing Him to breathe into me, to feel His power touch my soul, to bask in the light from His beautiful face, and to rest in His strong, secure arms—what on earth could be more important? As He breathes into me, I feel as though I am resurrected; and all the deep recesses within me that are dry and dead are suddenly revived. Peace enters in and drives out chaos.

What a wondrous miracle we are permitted to experience: God, the Lord of all, Who created all things, desires to live within us and breathe into us! Truly, I cannot "live by bread alone, but by every word that comes from the mouth of God'" (Matt. 4:4). I need my intimate Friend desperately.

What a blessing to know that He is always waiting just a whisper away for me to call on Him. What a blessing that He is not pouting or waiting to punish my undulating dedication. What a blessing that He stands ever ready to sit with me and speak to me. And if I'm waiting for my life to settle down so that I can get my priorities right, I am waiting in vain. But as I make the choice to "'be still and know that [He is] God'" (Psalm 46:10), everything else will either fall into place or fade away to its proper level of importance.

Peter tells us that grace and peace come through intimacy. He greets fellow believers by saying, "May grace and peace be multiplied to you in the *knowledge* of God and of Jesus our Lord" (2 Peter 1:2, emphasis mine). Peace amid the storms of life—and even the worst persecution—is available to those whose roots have gone deep in the Lord, those who have made the effort to know Him intimately.

This is the promise of finding home with God. It is from this place of hiding away with the Lord that you will find peace and safety. "He who dwells in the shelter of the Most High will abide in the shadow of the Almighty . . . Because you have made the LORD your dwelling place—the Most High, who is my refuge—no evil shall be allowed to befall you, no plague come near your tent" (Psalm 91:1, 9-10). These are glorious promises to those who find their place in the shelter of God.

> *"Peace I leave with you; my peace I give to you. Not as the world gives do I give to you. Let not your hearts be troubled, neither let them be afraid."*
>
> John 14:27

AN ETERNAL PERSPECTIVE

When we spend time in the presence of the Lord, our perspective shifts. We cease to be all about the here and now and begin to see through the eyes of Heaven. We know Heaven is our destination, and it has stopped being a dimly lit, imaginary place. It is vibrant in its beauty and in its ability to bathe our earthly existence in its light.

Jesus said, "'And this is eternal life, that they know you, the only true God, and Jesus Christ whom you have sent'" (John 17:3). Having eternal life is about so much more than living forever; it is about knowing God in an intimacy so deep that His reality presses in on your reality, and your perspective is synced with His. We won't be strangers or casual acquaintances to Him when we, at long last, meet Him face to face in Heaven if we have been walking with Him all this time on earth.

When I go to His home permanently, it will be the continuation of the Divine dance, the culmination of the sweet romance He and I nurtured while I spun on this dying sphere.

> *"Yet I am always with you; you hold me by my right hand. You guide me with your counsel, and afterward you will take me into glory. Whom have I in heaven but you? And earth has nothing I desire besides you. My flesh and my heart may fail, but God is the strength of my heart and my portion forever."*
>
> Psalm 73:23-26 NIV

CHAPTER 6
TRANSFORMATIVE BENEFITS

FROM MY UPBRINGING, I KNEW the Lord spoke to people; but I thought it was limited to major incidents, the big decisions of life in which reason failed me or for the purpose of ministering to others. It had not really penetrated my thoughts that the Lord wanted to speak to me about everything. I knew His leading, but I was like a nearly blind and deaf animal, taking the Lord's leading more from bumps on the head I acquired by running into things than from learning to hear and respond to the voice of my Good Shepherd.

Many of us know Psalm 32:8, which says, "I will instruct you and teach you in the way you should go; I will counsel you with my eye upon you." However, few of us are as familiar with the verse that follows it directly and says, "Be not like a horse or a mule, without understanding, which must be curbed with bit and bridle, or it will not stay near you."

Did you catch that? In verse eight, the Lord says He will direct us through instruction, teaching, and counsel that comes directly from Him and His intimate acquaintance with us. In verse nine, He encourages us to not be like a pack animal that needs to be pulled by a bit or bridle to communicate where it is to go. This animal will wander if it is not constantly kept in check because it's only paying attention to the circumstances that bump it around instead of listening to the voice of its Master. A pack animal may be obedient enough while connected to the bit and bridle, but it is without an understanding of the plans and purposes of its Master. There is no companionship between a pack animal and the Master. God wants more with us than that type of relationship; He wants companionship.

God wanted to pull me from simply being led by what I bumped into and draw me into intimate companionship with Himself. It took effort to press in for a deeper relationship while I still had haunting misconceptions that "you either had it, or you didn't," like hearing from God was something you were born with. I was afraid I was one who was just destined to live on the fringe. I had no choice in the matter. Occasionally, the Lord would give me words of wisdom for people at church; but I longed for more, for something more intimate, for a place where I knew I was welcomed and wanted and cherished. I wanted a relationship with the Lord that had nothing to do with other people.

I wrote this in my journal twenty years ago:

> *I've been meditating on Exodus 33:12b-13a. "You [God] have said, 'I know you [Moses] by name, and you have also found favor in my sight.' Now therefore, if I have found favor in your sight, please show me now your ways, that **I may know you** in order to find favor in your sight." [emphasis mine] It's almost as if Moses is saying, "You know me—that's great, but I want to know You, too! In order for me to really know You, I have to learn Your ways." How exactly does one go about that?*
>
> *I know reading the Word is part of that—a big part. But Moses didn't have the Bible. How did he do it? . . . I felt the Lord tell me to read John 12 and John 8. I did and was very encouraged to see much of them talked about knowing God . . . John 12:45-46 really stuck with me. It reads, "And whoever sees me sees him who sent me. I have come into the world as light, so that whoever believes in me may not remain in darkness."' It's almost as if Jesus is saying He is the Light Who enables us to see and know the Father. In John 8:19b, Jesus says, "'If you knew me, you would know my Father also.'"*

WISDOM

Some may think that to be intellectual and use the reason God gave them is the highest calling of man. It is not; relationship is the highest calling. In fact, Scripture makes it clear that when religion is devoid of relationship, wisdom will leave. Look at what the Lord says in Isaiah 29:13-14: "Because this people draw near with their mouth and honor me with their lips, while their hearts are far from me, and their fear of me is a commandment taught by men, therefore, behold, I will again do wonderful things with this people, with wonder upon wonder; and the wisdom of their wise men shall perish, and the discernment of their discerning men shall be hidden." When your relationship with the Lord is reduced to lip service, even the wisdom you pride yourself on will evaporate.

Human wisdom is foolishness compared to the wisdom of God (1 Cor. 3:19); and for the person who longs to live a life characterized by wisdom, this intimate communication with the Lord is where a ready resource of wise counsel is found.

In Daniel 2:28 and 47, God is twice described as a Revealer of mysteries. There is no better place to turn when you need revelation than to the One Who desires to help you walk in wisdom. God promises, "Call to me and I will answer you, and will tell you great and hidden things that you have not known" (Jer. 33:3).

God speaks to His children, as He always has. He did not abandon His children at any point in history. Getting to a place where you can hear the Lord is not quick and easy. It requires more than desire; it requires effort. But never mistakenly believe that because something requires effort, it is impossible or not for you. I am convinced that many give up just short of success. God does speak, and His Word promises that He will give us wisdom when we ask (James 1:5).

Never compartmentalize your intimate relationship with the Lord apart from daily activities. Retain in your conscious mind that God is always with you and tangible and do not allow God to be relegated, even for a short time, to your subconscious. Do not consign seeking the Lord's wisdom to areas of major concern. Seek Him for even the smallest questions of what to do.

You will find that the Holy Spirit has wisdom to offer you on the most minor details of life. No question is too small; no question of how things work is too beneath Him to answer. I know many people who will say, "The Lord doesn't care if you get the red car or the blue car! He's not interested in the tiny, inconsequential details!" While it is quite true that it does not matter at all to the Kingdom of God what color your car is, the Holy Spirit can tell you what you will be happy with in the long run.

Please understand that I'm not saying that you should consult God and then sit around and wait for the answer at every intersection of life. A moving ship is easier to steer; and often, He has already deposited the desire for certain things in your heart. And that is how you will know what He wants you to do. When answers are self-evident, God does not want us to sit around and wait for some heavenly light show to point the way He has already planted in your spirit.

If you desire to live life with wisdom, ask the One Who has all wisdom. You will live wiser. You will begin to see how He sees, and you will grow in wisdom. You will see what is important to Him, and your heart will change. You can also lay aside the stress of thinking you should have done things differently as you rest in the knowledge that you have done as you were told and things will work out.

> *"If any of you lacks wisdom, let him ask God, who gives generously to all without reproach, and it will be given him."*
>
> James 1:5

INQUIRING VERSUS SEEKING

When we speak of intimacy with God, we are speaking of a relationship that goes deeper than laying out our petitions. This distinction is seen in the Word of God as well. "'I will stretch out my hand against . . . those who have turned back from following the LORD, who do not seek the LORD or inquire of him'" (Zeph. 1:4, 6). Notice there is a distinction between seeking the Lord and inquiring of Him. Those who "inquire of the Lord" are those who are asking the Lord a question, while those who "seek the Lord" are those who pursue past finding answers to problems; they pursue a relationship with the Lord Himself. We have to transcend a surface-level relationship to develop intimacy.

We need to seek Him beyond just wanting to hear from Him on things pertaining to us. We need to quiet ourselves enough to get our own needs and desires out of the way and focus solely on our Lord and His will. Spend time in simple adoration of the One your heart desires.

> *"Truly, truly, I say to you, you are seeking me, not because you saw signs, but because you ate your fill of the loaves. Do not work for the food that perishes, but for the food that endures to eternal life, which the Son of Man will give to you."*
>
> John 6:26-27

JOY

Having an intimate relationship with the Creator brings more joy than any other human experience. We were created for this place of belonging to God, so it makes sense that it is where we will find our deepest joy. To know that you are known and adored by the Father and that He has provided the way for you to enter into His holy presence through the sacrifice of His own Son's blood will captivate your spirit and bind you to the heart of God.

Joy is also the natural by-product of the peace that fills your heart when you intimately know your Abba and trust Him implicitly. The ability to cast your cares on the Lord because you know without a doubt that He cares for you (1 Peter 5:7) removes burdens from your life. It will give you a lightness in your heart and mind where there used to be the weight of thinking you have to do and care for things in your own strength.

Often, we have a misconception of God as being angry, or at least super-serious. We view Him with a consternated frown of displeasure or worry. But our God is not worried! When you give your worries and burdens to Him, He does not sit on His throne and begin fretting over them. No, He is at peace. In Nehemiah 8:10, we are told that the joy of the Lord is our strength. That doesn't just mean that when we are joyful, God is strong for us. It means that there is a type of joy that belongs to the Lord. It is His joy; and when we are intimate with Him, we are permeated with His type of joy. We will find supernatural strength when we are permeated with this supernatural joy. It comes through being close enough to the Lord to allow Him to take up our cares and to see how calmly He takes them in hand. This joy is the confident assurance that nothing is too hard for our God, and we are safely in His hands while He works it out.

Most of us forget that the Lord is truly joyful over us. We tend to think He looks on us through the microscope of displeasure, yet Zephaniah says, "The LORD your God is in your midst, a mighty one who will save; he will rejoice over you with gladness; he will quiet you by his love; he will exult over you with loud singing" (3:17).

The Lord delights in you; He is blessed by you. And when you feel the joy of His presence, you are tasting a bit of the joy He has in you.

> *"For you make him most blessed forever;*
> *you make him glad with the joy of your presence."*
>
> Psalm 21:6

CHRISTLIKENESS

Living in the United States, our responsibility to vote is profound. Men and women died so that we could exercise the right. But sometimes, it is exasperating to also have to endure the onslaught from the media, the ads, and the phone calls. On more than one occasion, it has made me contemplate the fact that all the politicians want is my vote. I sure wish the politicians wanted more than my vote. I'm afraid most of them have forgotten, and some have never grasped that what they should really want is to make a difference, to change the world for the better, to reinstate the original vision for our nation, to make this country a more hospitable place for the helpless and a less hospitable place to those who would do us harm.

Often, it seems they just want to fill a slot, to have a job, to take up another term. In our government, our elected officials are our representatives. Did you catch that? *Our* representatives. That means they had better not go off to Washington and start acting the fool and doing underhanded deals. They represent me! They better be men and women of integrity and be constantly watching those of us who put them in office for what *we* want them to do.

This is not tremendously unlike God, Who elects us and then sends us into the world to represent Him. What kind of representatives are we? Are we watching Him to make sure that we are doing what He wants us to be doing? Are we reflecting Him accurately, or are we doing our own shady deals to get things done? I hope the Lord finds us to be men and women of integrity, who do what we say we will do in a fashion that reflects His heart and purposes.

It is not enough to occasionally invoke the name of God and call that an accurate representation. It is even worse to say you belong to Him and then act for yourself more often than for Him. Is this not what some of our governmental "representatives" do that so galls us?

Who do we represent? Do we say we represent God, but then make Him out to be an angry, vengeful terror? Do we represent Him as a cosmic fool, Who is so codependent on us that we can mock and ridicule obedience and devotion to Him as He simply rolls over and tells us to do it again? And thus, the old paganism is revived again as we form God into our own images instead of knowing that we are made in *His* image and striving to form ourselves into His likeness.

But we are believers in the one, true Sovereign God, Who has a definite way of being. It's not our choice Who He is or how He acts. We must represent Him as He is, not as we would like Him to be to fit our agendas.

He is a forgiving and loving God Who desires that no one perish. He is the One Who is always there for us, Who wants us to come into a saving knowledge of Him. He is the One Who will then carry us from an infant faith into a maturity that will represent Him well. He is the One Who will help us grow up, even when it is uncomfortable to our flesh—not because He likes to see us squirm but because He is committed to seeing us leave behind the things we thought would make us happy to find those things that will truly fulfill.

This is the God we need to be representing. But how can we ever represent God accurately if we do not know Him intimately? Getting in His presence, hearing His heart, sharing our own, and letting Him refine us—these are the ways in which we are molded into knowing God's true character and then representing Him to the world around us. The head knowledge we can get about God secondhand (through teaching and books) is valuable, but nothing can take the place of firsthand knowledge that transforms our hearts to His image. This is only available through soaking in His Word and in His presence.

"Therefore be imitators of God, as beloved children."

Eph. 5:1

CHAPTER 7
BEING KNOWN

COMPANIONSHIP GOES BOTH WAYS: WE know someone, and we are fully known. Many are less comfortable with this aspect of intimacy. As we have touched on, we acquired this fear of being fully known in the Fall. Prior to the Fall, God and man enjoyed unblemished intimacy. No stain of sin hampered the relationship. And as we have already discussed, we inherited the same instinct as Adam—to cover up and hide from God.

We can see this play out in the life of Jacob in the twenty-seventh chapter of Genesis. Jacob wants the blessing of his father. In order to get it, he must get close to his father. He pretends to be his older brother Esau in his elaborate ruse to get the desired blessing.

As a result of the Fall and our desire to hide who we really are, many of us would prefer to do as Jacob did. We attempt to deceive the Father by pretending to be what we are not in His presence, maintaining a facade that keeps God at arm's length, never letting Him see the secret places of our hearts. Jacob tied goatskins to his arms to appear hairy like his brother and pulled on his brother's clothing to smell like him, tricking his blind father. We try to look different than we are, but we do not serve a blind Father. Our God knows all the truth about us already and is not the least surprised by the real you. Trying to tell Him what you think He wants to hear is a fruitless effort and will keep you going in circles until you are transparent with yourself and with God. Jacob, the deceiver, was out-deceived by his uncle Laban and went in circles until he was ready to face up to his deception and come home.

Just as salvation, though initiated by God, must be a choice of our will, so must intimacy be something we choose. God initiates the longing in our hearts, but He does not force this relationship upon us. We see this at the Fall. God knows full well where Adam is and yet chooses to wait and ask, "Adam, where are you?" God is asking for access to Adam's heart.

If you sense the prompting of God asking, "Where are you?" answer Him right now. Give Him access to all your secret places. Refuse to do the natural thing and hide. Do the supernatural thing and come into the warmth of His light and find love.

KNOWN AND HEARD

Shortly before Christmas years ago, I came down with bronchitis. Unlike my dear husband who can work a full day and go to the gym while sick and still improve, my world has to stop. Trying to make my world stop as Christmas approaches is laughable! So, just as my antibiotics ran out, my fever came back; and we decided that I should truly get some rest.

The only problem was that the following day, I was scheduled to babysit three of my grandchildren the whole day, so our daughter and son-in-law could celebrate their anniversary! Graciously, our middle daughter offered to take my place as babysitter, despite it being her first day back from college. My hubby also took the day off to ensure I stayed in bed, far away from the babies.

As I lay upstairs in my bed reading, I could hear my precious grandchildren come through the front door. Just the sounds of their voices made it difficult to stay sequestered. I could hear them downstairs talking excitedly to their auntie, whom they call Scoop.

"Look, Auntie Scoop," one said as he examined the Christmas tree, "I see a red blueberry!"

"It's a strawberry," she answered gently.

"Here's another!" he exclaimed.

Our granddaughter, with her softer voice that is always highlighted by little squeaks, said, "Let's go look at Baby Jesus!"

Oh, how the sound of their voices thrilled me! The oldest, at only five years old, sounded so much like his mommy did, even though he is a boy. When I couldn't see his handsome, little face, the sound of his voice threw me into a time warp! All that has changed now that he is in his teens and his voice has grown deeper. But back then, I closed my eyes and listened as visions came back to me of a precious little, brown-eyed girl with dark brown, bobbed hair who could pack each waking moment with drama and exuberance.

The Lord whispered to me of His infinite love for each of us and the thrill He has of hearing our voices. As Matthew chapter seven shows, if we, as fallible parents, desire any good thing for our children, it is only a small glimpse of how our Father desires to do great things for us! What an awesome God, Who loves us so dearly and longs to just hear the sound of our voices!

At some point during that long-ago day, our oldest grandson got upset; and I could faintly hear him from my room upstairs speaking to his auntie in a crying voice. It may sound dramatic; but it rent my heart, and I felt tears come to my eyes. I so wanted to comfort, to intervene, to help. How much more must our Abba be moved with compassion as we cry out to Him in our hurts, pains, and frustrations? Rest assured, He is moved.

God hears every word, every cry, and every sigh. He is intimately acquainted with all that affects you. The man who was born blind and healed by Jesus declared that it is common knowledge that "if anyone is a worshiper of God and does his will, God listens to him" (John 9:31). Think about that: God listens to worshipers who obey Him.

We serve a God Who says, "No longer do I call you servants . . . but I have called you friends" (John 15:15). Friends have "give and take" and intimacy that others have no access to. I share things with my closest friends that I know better than to share with those outside that safe closeness. They do the same with me. If it were not mutual, it would not be friendship. Yet the Lord calls us His friends.

Consider Abraham's conversation with the Lord in Genesis 18 when Abraham is appealing to the Lord on behalf of the few righteous people in Sodom and Gomorrah. That type of communication—where God is standing still to listen to a human being—is available only to all who are in the type of friendship that gives "confidence to enter the holy places by the blood of Jesus, by the new and living way that he opened for us" (Heb. 10:19-20). It is a relationship of mutual accessibility.

Lift your voice to your Abba today! Lift your voice and offer to Him whatever is in your heart. Give Him your pains. Give Him praise. Most of all, give Him the gift of just hearing you speak to Him.

> *"I love the LORD, because he has heard my voice and my pleas for mercy. Because he inclined his ear to me, therefore I will call on him as long as I live."*
>
> Psalm 116:1-2

PURSUING CONVERSATIONAL COMPANIONSHIP WITH GOD

When I speak of companionship, I am not suggesting God is a silent Partner, as Someone Who quietly resides in your heart's home but seldom has anything to say. Conversational companionship is the heart of God. He longs to have a conversational relationship with each and every one of His children. God speaks, and His speaking is the clear indication telling you He desires fellowship with you, a two-way interaction. His heart's desire is for you to realize He knows you completely and loves you absolutely, and He also desires for you to come to know Him and love Him.

I wish I could say this journey is an easy one. It is not. As easy as it is to fall in love, it takes effort to make a relationship grow, to continue making the effort to connect, to speak and to listen. This relationship is no different.

As a young person, I was certainly in love with my Abba, and I was in love with being in love. But actually pursuing Him took tenacity.

If you want this relationship, you have to decide if you want it at any cost. You are going to have to pursue it like a lover willing to overcome every obstacle the world can throw at you. This type of relationship is not available to the casual lover who only wants to flirt and have fun. Pursuing God takes more than an "easy come, easy go" attitude.

But once you have experienced this kind of love, nothing else matters. You will never be able to settle for anything less.

A PLACE FOR TWO

Knowing God is an individual thing. No one can have a relationship with God on your behalf. You do not arrive at intimacy based on the merit of another's relationship with the Lord. This home of companionship was built for two.

Take for illustration the parable of the ten virgins, which we find in Matthew 25:1-12. In this parable, there are ten people who are waiting for the bridegroom to arrive for the wedding feast. Five of them brought extra oil for their lamps in case the groom was a long time coming; five brought only enough oil to keep their lamps lit for the amount of time they assumed they would have to wait. That oil is indicative of intimacy.

Sure enough, their initial supply of oil burned hot and bright but soon burned out, leaving the five without reserve supply watching their flames flicker and go out. They wanted to borrow oil from the first five. But each one's oil was her own. It could not be shared, just as intimacy with the Lord is not a commodity that can be experienced vicariously.

The five who had run out of oil had no choice but to leave their waiting place and purchase more oil. While they were gone, the bridegroom arrived, welcoming in the five who were waiting with their lamps lit and leaving the five who had run out excluded from the party.

When the five who left to purchase oil returned, they pleaded, "'*Lord, lord, open to us.*' But [the bridegroom] answered, '*Truly, I say to you, I do not know you*'" (vv. 11-12).

It is those who live in readiness through companionship with the Lord who are the ones able to enter the wedding feast. The rest hear the haunting words, "I never knew you."

FRIEND AND COUNSELOR

Diving into companionship with the Creator and Perpetuator of the universe is a beautiful and intimate thing. It is also something magnificently bigger than ourselves. It may be both more personal and more global than you have imagined.

Job described his relationship with the Lord when he mourned its loss, saying, "Oh, that I were as in the months of old . . . as I was in my prime, when the friendship of God was upon my tent" (29:2, 4). That last phrase could literally be translated, "'when God's council was by my tent,' or 'when God was an intimate in my tent.'"[3] Our deepest desire should be for Him to make His habitation with us; to have a perpetual, continually growing, vibrant companionship; and to have God call us His friend.

Ironically, in Job 15:8, Job's "friend" Eliphaz questions Job and almost mockingly challenges, "Have you listened in the council of God?" The truth was Job did indeed have an intimate relationship with God, which involved him interacting in the council of God. Though a companion of God, Job did not know everything that went on in Heaven; and faith was still required in the relationship.

In Job's final speech, after God had answered him, he says, "I had heard of you by the hearing of the ear, but now my eye sees you" (42:5). Job's trial brought a new and much deeper intimacy. All trials present a crossroads of

---

[3] Kenneth L. Barker, General Editor, *NIV Study Bible*, Study Notes (Grand Rapids, Michigan: Zondervan, 2002), 760.

decision: fall away or grow even more deeply rooted. Our relationship with the Father can be like the "intimate friendship" Job had.

David speaks of his relationship with God, saying, "The friendship of the LORD is for those who fear him, and he makes known to them his covenant" (Psalm 25:14). What an amazing concept to realize: God confides in human beings!

Nevertheless, David was not unique. His son, Solomon, also testified to this reality when he said, "The upright are in [the Lord's] confidence" (Prov. 3:32). And God spoke this truth through the prophet Amos. "For the Lord GOD does nothing without revealing his secret to his servants the prophets" (Amos 3:7).

The Hebrew word used in each of these verses and translated "friendship," "confidence," and "secret" is the word *sode*. This word means, "a *session*, that is, *company* of persons (in close deliberation); by implication *intimacy, consultation, a secret*: - assembly, counsel, inward, secret (counsel)."[4]

This is why it is so vital that we look beyond ourselves in our intimate times with the Lord. It's not all about us! Once we are able to truly adapt to this truth and get over ourselves, we are available to sit in on the council of the Lord, to hear His plans about the bigger picture, to hear His heart for others.

What a remarkable revelation! We, too, can be taken into God's confidence like David, Solomon, and Amos. If this relationship was available to those in the Old Testament era when the Holy Spirit was only on a few people for a limited time, how much more it is available to us under the New Covenant, who have been gifted with the Holy Spirit, the Counselor, as a resident within us.

> *"Let us know; let us press on to know the LORD; his going out is sure as the dawn;*
> *he will come to us as the showers, as the spring rains that water the earth."*
>
> Hosea 6:3

---

[4] James Strong, *New Strong's Exhaustive Concordance* (Nashville: Thomas Nelson Publishers, 1996), s.v. "sode."

CHAPTER 8
A FRUIT-FILLED LIFE

I HAVE A GREAT IMAGINATION. I ascribe this in part to my childhood. I was the youngest of four, and we loved pretending. However, they all outgrew it long before I did, so I ended up playing a lot of pretend on my own—and playing all the parts! Sometimes, I would pretend, and the boy would win the heart of the fair maiden. They would get married and simply live happily ever after. However, more often than not, it couldn't end there for me. There was still another romantic adventure that would complete the story—baby would make three.

As a young girl, my grandest ambition second to finding my great love was to become a mommy—to nurture and love a sweet, soft somebody of my own. I made my feminist fourth grade teacher so mad, she called my mother in for a conference when she heard that being a wife and mother was my goal in life. One year, my big brother queried me on what I had asked for from Santa after we had visited him at the mall.

When I told him I had asked for a dolly, he, in masculine mystification, exclaimed, "You ask for that every year!"

True enough. Though we never had much money, I always had several "babies." I was practicing for my dream come true.

Just as it is the core desire for most of us to have a "happily ever after," it is followed by another core desire—to have children. Ideally, children make a completeness in life that few other achievements can. To give life to another human being that will live on after you and will hopefully have children that will live on after them is a thrilling prospect. It is legacy. It is what makes you continue on this planet long after you have left it.

Spiritually speaking, if we are to have intimacy with the Lord, we must expect, desire, and open ourselves to produce offspring. We must bear children. There must be fruit.

This is true in the corporate setting. If we are part of a church body that is intimate with the Lord, we will naturally produce spiritual children. New believers and those who crave what we have will be drawn to us. We will not be able to stop it. Intimacy is attractive.

This is also true as individual believers. There should be enough fruit in our lives that others are drawn by what they see. Perhaps the average person won't comprehend exactly what draws them, but they will be drawn, nonetheless. As with Moses when his face glowed from the presence of the Lord, so should it be with us. People should be able to say, "I can see that you have been with the Lord." Our faces should "glow"—not in some pious, "holier than thou" way depicted in Renaissance art but in an inexplicable, intangible way. Spiritually, we should look different.

Fruit is the result of intimacy. We cannot bypass intimacy and hope for fruit some other way. Though fruit is not always the dramatic outcome of intimacy, there is no way to have fruit without it. What is the fruit of the intimacy you have with the Lord? What is the growth that is occurring in your life? What changes are you experiencing? Has God given you a "baby"?

When God created Adam and Eve in the garden, He blessed them and then instructed them, saying, "'Be fruitful and multiply and fill the earth'" (Gen. 1:28). Just as God called His first human beings to be fruitful and multiply in the natural sense, so also He calls the first of His Church to do so spiritually. Just before Jesus' ascension, He met with them and instructed them, "'Go therefore and make disciples of all nations'" (Matt. 28:19).

"Be fruitful and multiply" and "go . . . and make disciples" are the same mandate—one at the inception of the natural world, the other at the inception of the New Covenant.

The fruit of intimacy is not for us alone. We must bear in mind that what we receive is intended to be shared and go on to ignite the fire of desire for God in another heart. Furthermore, it is in His presence that we are anointed to minister. It is there that we find the anointing, strength, and desire to reach out to all of God's children. As priests did not enter into the presence only for themselves and Jesus did not enter into the heavenly Holy of Holies for His own sake, neither should we be content to soak in the presence of God and then hide our blessed connection under a bushel, selfishly keeping the revelation of the open veil all to ourselves. There is no doubt that the one who presses forward to enter into the presence of God will be personally blessed; but if he has truly been with the Lord, he will desire what the Lord desires. His heart will be moved with what moves God's heart—people.

> *"Then the angel showed me the river of the water of life, bright as crystal, flowing from the throne of God and of the Lamb through the middle of the street of the city; also, on either side of the river, the tree of life with its twelve kinds of fruit, yielding its fruit each month. The leaves of the tree were for the healing of the nations."*
>
> Rev. 22:1-2

PAST THE ATTRACTION PHASE

Do you believe in love at first sight? I guess I would *like* to believe in it—that one and only person created for you catches your eye, and you are forever blissfully in love. And though I do believe in attraction at first sight, I would not call that "love." After being married as long as I have, I realize that love—real love—is something that cannot happen in an instant, no matter how attracted you may be. True love would mean knowing and then, with all you know about that other person, still loving.

We tend to think the same way about God. We are touched by Him, and we are never the same. But perhaps that is only the attraction stage. And then, without ever getting to truly know Him, we profess our love and go on our merry way, believing that we have all we need. Now, I am not saying that you are not instantly changed and saved through faith in the grace God extends through the life of His Son, Jesus. Salvation is like that first look, but we should want more than goosebumps and heart palpitations. We should want *yada*—intimate knowing, companionship. Companionship only comes in the context of a relationship—a connection that involves communication.

I'm afraid that too often, we are satisfied with the inoculation of our first sight of God and never get saturated enough with Him to fall head over heels in that "knowing love." We are too content to have the "Christian" label without the heart-altering branding of Him searing deeply into our souls, forever changing us at our most core level. That branding smells too much of our flesh burning, of letting go of what was familiar and opening ourselves to the potential of not running our own lives. We seek, after all, to hold tightly to our lives, thinking we are saving them, only to see that what we held to has perished in our asphyxiating grasp; and what we could have had, if we had let go of our control, was glorious life.

Let's not be like Naomi's daughter-in-law, Orpah, who voiced allegiance and kissed with transient passion but then turned and walked away (Ruth 1:14-15). Let us instead be as Ruth, who clung to the things of God, knowing that her true life was dependent upon her letting go of all she had known and taking hold of the God of Israel (Ruth 1:16-17). In doing so, she, in turn, gave new life—to Naomi, to Boaz, to Obed, to the very lineage of Jesus.

What is waiting for us if we would simply let go of the seemingly safe ledge to which we are clinging and dive into all God is and all He has for us?

So many just want a taste, a safe glance at the glory and majesty of God. I sat and chatted a while ago with a man who boasted that his church just taught the love and grace of God. "You know, nothing too hard," he said, beaming, little knowing it is some of the harder things we learn that become a true foundation under our feet. We will need that type of firm foundation when the earth commences its habitual shaking.

How sorrowful to be perpetually engaged and never consummate the marriage, to flirt eternally with God when He is holding out to us the wedding ring and the associated unbreakable covenant. Why do we want just a taste when we could be filled?

Being close to God will often cause a conception. A seed will be planted deep inside you. Something will take root in you that you always knew was possible but that you have never before experienced. The seed of God and a dream that has been waiting in you will come together to create life. You knew there was an empty place. God had created the empty place—not to leave it empty but that it might be filled with His dream for you. You were created with an abiding desire, something that cried out to be made complete. Perhaps, you unsuccessfully tried to make it complete on your own. It will not be complete until you find your place with God—that intimate place—that the seed will be able to pass to you to bring life to that dream.

> *"When Rachel saw that she bore Jacob no children, she envied her sister. She said to Jacob, 'Give me children, or I shall die!'"*
>
> Gen. 30:1

PART 3
CHALLENGES TO CONQUER

CHAPTER 9
FEELING UNWORTHY

I LOVE GAZING AT THE night sky. The fingerprints of God across the heavens thrill me. Living all of my adult life in a large metropolis means that whenever I get out of town, my eyes are drawn heavenward, to the blinking, shooting, brilliant, and dim stars above me. I still remember my eighth-grade science class and learning about the phases of the moon.

Super moons are particularly captivating. A super moon occurs when the moon is unusually close to the earth and appears larger and more brilliant than normal. Scientists say that in the week that follows the super moon, there are some pretty interesting tides—nothing to worry about, but of course, the gravitational pull of the moon is reflected in the tides of the seas.

Sometimes, I feel something like a gravitational pull on my heart. I know it comes from something outside me, something bigger than me. There are times I feel a deep longing in my heart for God—just to reach out and grab hold of Him, to hear Him whisper my name, to voice a praise, to be on my face before Him. This is not because of my stellar human nature. We must come to recognize that every drawing we feel is only a response to God's pull on us. His desire for us is so much stronger than the strongest of our desires for Him. It is *His* longing that inspires ours. He initiates fellowship.

So many times, when we sense that pulling, we ignore it. We each have our reasons: busyness, the distractions of this world, ignorance of the possibilities of fellowship with the Lord, or a guilty conscience. Yet nothing should keep us from that glorious experience of intimate fellowship. We must trust in the One Who desires us. We must trust in the One Who made it possible. We must trust in the One Who removed every stain and declares us righteous. We must exercise our faith and enter in.

I am determined that when I feel that pull, I will respond. I will not dodge or neglect or make excuses. "I am my beloved's and my beloved is mine" (Song of Songs 6:3). I will be as the tide—willingly and helplessly swayed by the lure of a Force of Love tugging at my heart. When I sense Him whisper my name, I will draw near and enter in.

Despite my deep desire for God, I find other things at work in my life that work against my desire for Him. This is where my insecurities play a role.

SHAME

Both of my parents gave their hearts to Jesus when I was two years old. They were filled with the zeal of new believers. It was great! Because of them, I knew God loved me and that I could have (and did have) my own, individual relationship with Him. I knew He knew all my actions and motives and thoughts. I knew I could talk to Him at any time, and He would hear me. What faded like a dream as I grew older was the idea that God wanted to talk back!

As I entered my teens, I continued to speak to God through prayer; and I believed He would somehow communicate with me on the big things. But I lost all expectations of daily companionship. It wasn't until my twenties that it began to dawn on me that God wanted to speak to my heart every day about the mundane as well as the monumental!

Largely, it was shame and a desire for control that entered my life, causing such backward movement in my relationship with the Lord. In my formative years, I turned to the Lord often, through abuses and hurts and fears. I turned to Him also in joys and celebrations. But I was filled with insecurities and fears of being alone, unloved, and unlovable. In my early teens, I doubted the Lord had my best interest at heart when it came to the direction my life was going (or at least how I, with the "infinite wisdom" of a fourteen-year-old, perceived it was going). I attempted to take control of my life to make it what I thought I wanted. This meant taking control away from my loving Lord and making an utter mess of things.

Much like the prodigal son, I found myself in a pit of my own making, in an abusive relationship, feeling more unloved and unlovable than ever. But I still retained the memory that my Abba loved me. I remember vividly a moment when I was sixteen, sitting on the edge of a bed in utter despair of my life with my Bible in hand, begging the Lord to rescue me. He graciously showed me His arms were still open wide, and He was waiting and watching for me, just like the Father in the parable (Luke 15:11-24). I ran home to Him. Graciously, He killed the fatted calf for me (figuratively speaking) in celebration as I committed to Him as I never had before.

I loved Him passionately. I was that woman who had been forgiven much and loved much (Luke 7:47). I could feel His gentle hands carry me in my weakness and bring me into wholeness.

And even though I knew intellectually my sin had been forgiven, I needed a revelation of my purity before God before I could move into close companionship with Him. I could never get close to Him if I still felt dirty and unworthy.

When we are more aware of our sin than of the blood of Jesus Christ which removes our sin, relationship will remain superficial. But provided we have repented of our sin, there is no reason at all that we should not "with confidence draw near to the throne of grace, that we may receive mercy and find grace to help in time of need" (Heb. 4:16).

Allowing sin to remain a barrier between yourself and God plays right into the enemy's plan. Satan will remind you of your sin in order to attempt to get you right back to where Adam and Eve were—hiding in the midst of the garden. Instead, enjoy the garden that Jesus died to restore in you and praise God for His gracious forgiveness. As Jesus said to the woman caught in adultery, "'Go, and from now on sin no more'" (John 8:11).

Psalm 100 is so simple and sweet that we often underestimate its profundity. Take a look:

> Make a joyful noise to the LORD, all the earth! Serve the LORD with gladness! Come into his presence with singing! Know that the LORD, he is God! It is he who made us, and we are his; we are his people, and the sheep of his pasture. Enter his gates with thanksgiving, and his courts with praise! Give thanks to him; bless his name! For the LORD is good; his steadfast love endures forever, and his faithfulness to all generations.

Notice how much joy and gladness is encouraged in the presence of God! This is not the place to weep and wail and continually seek forgiveness for sins that have been taken away by the Lamb of God. This is not a place to beat yourself with the bludgeoning bat of your past; this is a place to rejoice that you are admitted entrance!

We serve a great and holy God, yet He wants intimate relationship with us. And we can have that relationship, not characterized by groveling but characterized by expressive joy! God is good. His love is never-ending, and our relationship is based on His faithfulness, not our worthiness.

In spite of anything you have done or been, by pursuing companionship with the Lord, you are not asking for something God is not wanting to give you. Not only is God the Source and the Answer to your longing, but also, remember that your longing is merely an imperfect reflection of *His* longing. The reason God gave you this longing was to give you a taste of His own. It is His own desire that we feel tugging at our hearts. It is the wooing of the Holy Spirit that causes the longing for a deeper, more intimate fellowship with our Father. Our human hearts are so fickle and changeable, and there is no good thing innately in them. Yet we see this good desire to draw near to God. This must be the very heart of God Himself transplanted within us by His Holy Spirit that we feel. He desires us to desire Him.

"This was according to the eternal purpose that he has realized in Christ Jesus our Lord, in whom we have boldness and access with confidence through our faith in him."

Eph. 3:11-12

RELINQUISHING CONTROL AND TRUSTING THE SHEPHERD

My other foundational reason for walking away from the Lord was my deep desire for control. I wasn't entirely sure He could be trusted with this one life of mine. As I returned to Him, I could see clearly that the control I desired by taking my life out of God's hands was the very catalyst to my life being out of control. Like a frightened child, I gradually placed the reins of control back in His hands.

Control is a hard thing to relinquish completely, and He and I played a gentle game of tug-of-war as I foolishly tested Him to see how much I could trust Him. My own attempts to maneuver my life in a direction I thought would make me happy had been disastrous; but I knew the Lord wanted everything from me, and I was afraid of what He would do if I gave it all to Him. In my immaturity, I didn't understand that when you give your all to the Lord, He gives His best for you, which far exceeds your own inferior dreams. If He calls you to do something, He gives you grace so that His call becomes the very thing you desire to do.

My twenties were largely spent in this awkward dance—the Lord shepherding and leading, while I followed cautiously, trying to retain the final veto right on any of His too-crazy plans. The conviction of that is seen in a prayer journal entry from my twenties. I had been studying Jacob, following his flight from Esau and his attempts to deceive people and keep the God of his father at arm's length. I wrote:

> *God continues to pursue Jacob, despite all his acts of deception and his conditional devotion to God. How many times do we "struggle with God" because we refuse to unconditionally accept God as our God and surrender to Him? How many times of meeting God face to face does it take to surrender ourselves totally? God has been pursuing me personally . . . for some time—meeting (me) face to face . . . (Am I) surrendered yet? (July 1997).*

All the while, I was quite in love with the Lord and learning more and more about Him. To lure me from my hiding places of shame and the desire for control, the Lord would continually bring people into my life who would give me glimpses of the "more of God" for Whom I desperately longed. These people would soon have me boiling over with godly jealousy! I wanted more of God actively working in my life, too! After all, my Abba had saved me out of my pit, out of the lowest place I had ever been! He saved me from that abusive relationship I thought would be better for me than the protection of His loving care. He brought me home to Himself and showed His love to me when I was at my lowest. Surely, there was a purpose for me.

In my prayer journal I wrote, "The Lord seems to be continually showing me something I want spiritually . . . but He doesn't give it to me. Then He shows me what it really would mean to have what I think I want and makes me decide if I'm really willing to have it. Only then does He give it to me! It is a continual process of surrender that is exciting and scary" (June 1997).

Pushing past shame and the desire for control is both exciting and scary. Something at our core desires being known. There is also an innate fear associated with this desire. To be known is the hope of acceptance but also the dread of rejection. The tendency to weave together fig leaves, as Adam and Eve did, persists today in the myriad of ways we cover up and hide from one another, from God, and even from ourselves. Trust can be a scary cure for what ails us, but it remains the only cure.

Why are there such intense hindrances to the development of this relationship? The enemy's worst fear is that you would develop this relationship. He knows that when you do, you will become an unstoppable force, no longer weighed down by doubt and fear and anxiety. He will try every tactic to keep you from growing in your depth of intimacy with the Lord. He will keep you stuck in the belief that you cannot trust the Lord fully and must retain some control of your life.

Knowing your Abba intimately and being in a position to continually receive wisdom, guidance, and reassurance from Him generates a confidence in which the enemy cannot get a foothold. You will now have the upper hand to overcome when the enemy tempts you to worry, fear, doubt, or willfully sin. Of course, Satan will fight this! By placing yourself in the secret place, you make yourself inaccessible to mental and emotional attack.

When the enemy uses the fear of relinquishing control as his mode of attack, he is operating in an illusory arena; it does not truly exist. It may be hard to hear, but you and I really do not have control over our lives. We cannot control what others do to us or the curveballs life sends our way. But the false belief that we can control our lives keeps us from trusting the Lord completely and taking full advantage of the comfort and safety He offers to those who put their trust in Him.

Fears are often a twist on reality that skews perspective to the enemy's advantage. It is vital that we remember this and keep it well-fixed in our minds as we battle in this arena. The more we focus on what is true, the better we will be able to defeat the fear and move forward.

> *"There is no fear in love, but perfect love casts out fear. For fear has to do with punishment, and whoever fears has not been perfected in love. We love because he first loved us."*
>
> 1 John 4:18-19

FEAR OF REJECTION

Walking this planet for any length of time, you will likely have picked up a few things. You may have picked up a past that prods you with shame or inadequacy or a history of feeling unwanted and excluded. Fear of rejection is one of the primary hindrances holding back so many of us with vulnerable hearts from jumping into the accepting arms of the Lord and receiving the love He has for us.

Regardless of where the fear of rejection originated, it generally taught us to be better at hiding than at intimacy. There can be no intimacy without revelation; and since we have discovered that revelation to the wrong person is dangerous, we hide. Yet we still desire the very thing we have made impossible: the complete acceptance that can only be realized by being fully known.

When Tim and I started dating many moons ago, we held our cards close to our chest, to some degree, putting on the nice face, the kind words, and pulling out all the stops when it came to romancing each other. We were not surprised that we liked each other! We rather liked ourselves, too, with our nice, attractive facades. But we wondered, "Will they like me when the facade evaporates, when I finally let them in and let them see the ugly that lurks inside?" We desperately wanted to know, but we feared the process of finding out.

We act similarly with the Lord. We begin to wonder if there is an impassable gap between our desire and the ability to see it fulfilled. We begin to think perhaps we have a desire that can never be realized.

But remember the nature of fear. Fear is not based in reality. The same is true for this ominous beast: rejection does not exist for the child of God. Here is the truth you need to grasp and hold onto in the very core of your being: You could never out-love God. You could never out-desire God. If you have any feelings of love or godly longing for another, it is not possible that you could have these virtues in greater measure than the One Who *is* Love!

He is the Ocean of love of which you feel merely a drip. God loves you. Get that in your core and walk in the splendor of knowing you are loved.

For those who have trusted in Jesus for salvation, we are His; and we have this promise: "It is the LORD your God who goes with you. He will not leave you or forsake you" (Deut. 31:6).

If you delve into the Hebrew for this Scripture, you will find that it says that *Yahweh*, the Ever-Present One, your God Himself walks right with you; He marches beside you.[5][6][7][8][9] He will never slacken or leave or fail you or be feeble and certainly never loosen or relinquish His grip on you or forsake you.[10] Armed with the knowledge of this type of unfailing love, we can defeat the fear of rejection and begin to experience all the love and acceptance our Abba has for us.

We have no need to hide like Adam and Eve or to alleviate our fear of rejection by interjecting an intermediary like the children of Israel at Mount Sinai. The hunger for fully exposed acceptance can never be met as long as we are hiding behind someone else and trying to slide into the presence of God by lurking in their shadow.

God wants you. He loves you. He adores you. He longs for closeness with you individually. Allow that love to drive out all fear so that you can partake in this relationship for which you were designed. This is the purpose for which you have been searching. Stop running and embrace the One Who already embraces you.

> *"For my father and my mother have forsaken me, but the LORD will take me in."*
>
> Psalm 27:10

---

5 James Strong, *New Strong's Exhaustive Concordance* (Nashville: Thomas Nelson Publishers, 1996), s.v. "Yahweh."
6 Ibid, s.v. "Hayah."
7 Ibid, s.v. "Halak."
8 Ibid, s.v. "Raphah."
9 Ibid, s.v. "Azab."
10 Jewish Publication Society, *The Tanakh* (Philadelphia: Jewish Publication Society, 2000).

VICTIM MENTALITY

Consider your human relationships and those around you who behave as victims. It is difficult to care for or love a victim enough. They are always demanding more. It is nearly impossible to love someone who does not want to heal because they would rather be able to lay out their hurts like treasured trinkets for all to see and admire.

The same is true in our relationship with the Lord. We may think that we want relationship and even pursue it; but unless we are willing to lay aside our victim badge and receive and trust the love the Lord gives, we will remain stuck in our identity as a victim. No matter how much healing love our Lord pours into us, we may choose neediness over healing and becoming responsible for ourselves. The victim mentality is tied inextricably to a need to control, for intimacy requires vulnerability. You must be willing to be disappointed or even hurt by others in order to lay down the desire to be the victim in a twisted illusion of control.

In the early days of my journey of intimacy with the Lord, there were days of progress when I felt the closeness of the Lord leading and guiding me; but they were sometimes few and far between. Some of my journal entries are essentially me whining before the Lord with the mindset of an unwanted victim. I felt like I was failing at this endeavor. Nevertheless, the Lord was patient. He never ceased wooing me. He continued to instruct, leading me to the Throne and into companionship.

One day, I was sitting in front of my overly crammed bookcase, reading a definition in my dictionary, when a book popped out of the bookcase and landed in my lap. I was shocked as I looked down to see a little green book I had inherited from my grandma's extensive library. At the time, I knew nothing about this book that would be pivotal in encouraging me in conversational relationship with the Lord. It was the classic book, *The Practice of the Presence of God* by Brother Lawrence, written in 1692.

I figured if the Lord was literally going to drop a book in my lap, I had better read it! As I did, I discovered the writings of a lowly monk who worked in a noisy kitchen at a monastery but who had committed himself to the Lord at such a deep heart level that he devoted himself to constant conversation with God. He had no victim mentality, in spite of the lowliness of his status, the challenges of his daily work, or his seeming failures at hearing from the Lord.

As I look back at journals and see my attempts at closeness, I clearly see now that God was speaking and directing. At the time I was striving, thinking I had to plead and prod and grovel to get God to speak to me. I didn't realize being still is enough. I was assailed by internal doubts, afraid companionship was reserved for the spiritually elite—pastors, evangelists, holy people of the past. I thought maybe I should just give up and try to have a "normal" life, comfortable and content, no longer straining so hard for Someone Who felt so elusive.

But my gracious Abba was shepherding me the whole time. And even more, I was sowing. My efforts looked like failures, but failing to hear in the manner I thought was necessary brought a desperation. In that desperation, the Lord gave me the glorious realization that I didn't have to strive and cajole to get my Father to talk to me. My musings left me with a private treasure trove documenting my journey and the Father never giving up. What I thought of as "failures" taught me to give my all while trusting God's desire to give me His best in His perfect love and timing.

> "Therefore do not throw away your confidence, which has a great reward. For you have need of endurance, so that when you have done the will of God you may receive what is promised."
>
> Heb. 10:35-36

CHAPTER 10
FEELING UNWILLING

I HATE BICEP CURLS. I do not know what it is about that one machine at the gym; but when I finally get the little seat adjusted and sit down, I just have the desire to lay my head down on the arm support and take a nap. I don't want to look stupid, though, so I stretch out my arms and take hold of the handles. Then I sit there staring through the window opposite me. I really don't feel like lifting the weight. I'm sure I sit there like that some days for a full thirty seconds before I muster my strength (and my realization that people are probably watching), and I finally lift the weight.

We all can find ourselves with an unwilling attitude when it comes to really pressing in and hearing from the Lord at times. There is a weight to be lifted, and it is important that I do it. I must flex these muscles I have been given and strengthen myself in the Lord.

Two things I know are true about this weightlifting: if I don't do it, I will get weaker; and if I do it, I will get stronger. But only I can do it. The same is true for pressing in to hear God. Though the Lord does the calling, it's up to me to choose to press in.

If I choose not to press in, I know it will seem even heavier when it comes my way tomorrow. If I decide that weightlifting is not a priority for me and I can forego the companionship of God, what a door I have opened—a door to floundering in the dark and doing things my way. However, if I choose to exercise this muscle, I have faith that one day, it won't be so heavy. And looking back, I can see my improvement and know this is true. I am so much better at it than I used to be. When I first started going to the gym, I could barely lift any amount of weight, and now what I used to work so hard to overcome is so light for me. But this comes only by choosing to lift today!

If I want the day to come when I can lift this weight without struggle, I must lift consistently. I must have faith that if I work at it, I will eventually see the gain. And the gain comes gradually, almost imperceptibly at times.

What keeps us in the rut of unwillingness, and what can we do to deal with it?

NOT WANTING "TOO MUCH"

Have you ever been scared to care too much, afraid your whole life could go sideways if you gave up control and immersed yourself in the things of God? I used to fear that I would become like some fanatic. "Best to keep just enough of God," I thought, "enough to keep me out of Hell but in with the 'right people.'"

Some time ago, my husband noticed that our pool was losing water. Water is automatically added to our pool every day, but it was not keeping up. When he mentioned it to me, I was concerned. What if we had a leak? We have a tree fairly close to the pool, and I have heard horror stories of the roots cracking pools in the search for water—not a pleasant prospect. Thankfully, it was just suddenly increasing temperatures, causing rapid evaporation.

We are all in constant need of filling, spiritually speaking, not just because of our human brokenness but because life is hard! Other people's brokenness hurt and disappoint us; our bodies sometimes seem to plot against us; and even natural disasters bring trouble and hardship into our lives. We get filled with strength from the Lord, but life's struggles evaporate it out of us. We need steady refilling from the Lord. It isn't enough to be filled occasionally; constant evaporation requires constant filling.

But is just getting neatly refilled with what you have lost enough for you? It is not enough for me. Somehow, I want more—more than daily refills, so much that it spills over to others I'm around. Trying to leash the Divine is a dangerous habit many of us have attempted in our fear of losing control of a God we know to be uncontrollable. We would rather get a weekly dose of strength each Sunday morning and leave our relationship at keeping God confined to a compartmentalized area of our lives. We would rather get just a taste than be flooded by His goodness or have Him require something of us.

I recently read the following quote by Wilbur Rees:

> I would like to buy $3 worth of God, please, not enough to explode my soul or disturb my sleep, but just enough to equal a cup of warm milk or a snooze in the sunshine... I want ecstasy, not transformation; I want the warmth of the womb, not a new birth. I want a pound of the Eternal in a paper sack. I would like to buy $3 worth of God, please.[11]

Oh, the tragedy of being so content with so little—to feel full, though you've not eaten, but barely unwrapped the packaging of God and tasted the surface! I want to gorge myself, to be filled to overflowing, to never be satisfied. I hope I never become some anorexic, abstemious Christian, pushing myself back from the feast laid before me, having only licked a few delicacies and smelled a few of the Chef's delights, dabbing a napkin at the corners of my mouth and politely saying, "Oh, that's enough. I know my limits. I have my girlish figure to consider."

Greedy? Yes, happily so. The very thought of being satisfied frightens me. I guess if I just wanted to maintain my level of fullness, there would be such a thing as "enough." But "enough" is not for me. I want overflowing because I have found a depth that is intoxicating, and I want more than

---

11 Wilber Rees, *$3 Worth of God* (Valley Forge: Judson Press, 1971), 5.

just enough for me. If I were just trying to be a cute, little swimming pool hidden away in a backyard, I would not want to overflow. But I want to be a river and carry what I have been given to others, to let them drink of the water that has filled me and get them hopelessly addicted to it. Oh, God, pour it on!

> *"They feast on the abundance of your house, and you give them drink from the river of your delights. For with you is the fountain of life; in your light do we see light."*
>
> Psalm 36:8-9

FEELINGS

Our flesh likes things it can perceive through the senses. Because God is a Spirit, you will be able to develop a relationship with Him primarily through your spirit. There will be times when you will perceive nothing in your flesh and must rely completely on what you perceive with your spirit. It is much easier for our fleshly selves to develop a relationship with people we can see and hear. We must be willing to make the effort to train our flesh to be in submission to our spirit. If we do not, our relationship will be merely based on the rarer occasions when our flesh can sense the Spirit. Goosebumps are nice, but they are flimsy things on which to build a relationship.

Believers whose relationships with the Lord are founded on feeling will never be stable. James tells us that one who has faith one moment and doubts the next "is a double-minded man, unstable in all his ways" (1:8). These poor, bedraggled souls will believe God loves them one day and think He hates them the next. Our foundation needs to be in something deeper than skin-deep feelings. It needs to be based in truth, knowing beyond a doubt Who the Father is and His heart for you.

Thankfully, the love and the presence of God are not based on our feelings. He is always available and present to us. He does not waiver in His love. He will never leave us, regardless of what our feelings may say.

> *"My soul is cast down within me;*
> *therefore I remember you."*
>
> Psalm 42:6

A FORM OF GODLINESS

I recently did a project in my house that involved painting all the door handles from their original polished brass to oil-rubbed bronze. I love it! It updated my house for the price of a can of spray paint. But please do not come to my house with sharp objects and start scraping on my handles. You would probably see polished brass peeking through.

I'm quite content with my fake makeover. I cannot promise I will be in ten years if it starts peeling; but for now, it makes me happy. If I had more money at my disposal, I may have just purchased new handles in the color I wanted, but this is great for now. Sometimes, being satisfied with a phony is fine, but the satisfaction usually only lasts for a time before the facade flakes away and reality comes haunting.

I have begun to ponder the different facades that may be in other areas of life and wonder why we would ever allow ourselves to be satisfied with them. Simply singing songs about God is not satisfying when we could allow our hearts to worship in the throne room of Heaven. Snacking on the Word of God is not enough when He desires to lay out a feast before us and be our Daily Bread. Presenting prayers like grocery lists falls far short of rejoicing in the realization that the God of the universe desires a deep, intimate relationship with us in all our humanness.

Rehoboam, the son of the richest king in the world who had brought peace to all of Israel, was, by his own foolish pride, plunged into continual war and poverty from the outset of his reign. The Word of God tells us that there was constant war with the ten tribes of Israel, who tore themselves away from Rehoboam's tribe of Judah and the Benjaminites (1 Kings 14:30). Though Rehoboam humbled himself after the initial losses, he allowed pride to grow again and abandoned God. Then the Egyptians ransacked Judah and even took the set of golden shields that Solomon had made. Sadly, Rehoboam could do little but replace the gold shields with bronze replicas.

It is hard to believe he was happy and content with replacing gold for bronze. Are we okay with the phonies in our lives? Maybe they are fine for a while; but eventually, the emptiness of it all will begin to gnaw at our satisfaction. The sooner, the better, I say. There is a blessed dissatisfaction when we finally see our fakes for what they are. The real thing is infinitely better. Whether that "real thing" is knowing God for Who He truly is or developing an authentic relationship with Him, that truth and authenticity is readily available to whomever is willing to reach out and grasp it.

A "religion" in which man attempts to create a god is empty, but so is worshipping the real God without recognizing that He is not a god of your own making. He is infinite and unchangeable and completely transcends the boxes we try to build around Him. Do not sit back and choose contentment with some version of Christianity that denies the power and the presence of God. Go for the real thing—relationship.

> *"For people will be ... having the appearance of godliness,*
> *but denying its power."*
>
> 2 Tim. 3:2, 5

CONFUSING FAITH WITH EXPECTATIONS

Many of us may have to wrestle with unrealistic expectations. We may expect a "third heaven" experience (2 Cor. 12:2) or a vision akin to the Revelation of John. Rather, here's the fine line we must walk: we must live expecting God to act but not set ourselves up for disappointment by expecting God to act as *we* have told Him.

I say this from personal experience. I have never had a problem believing for huge miracles. This may sound quite silly, but when I was a young girl, I stood at the steps of our family's swimming pool and tried for hours to walk on water. Yep, it's true. It isn't that I thought I was that special. No, I just thought I had the faith to do it!

At another time, I was going through a rather desperate time in my teens and cried out to God for an outrageously miraculous sign. I sat for hours and just waited. Nada. Nothing. Zilch. Bupkis. Honestly, I felt pretty dejected afterward. Had God not seen my amazing faith? But somehow, God continued to give me the strength to continue.

On the one hand, I had faith that God could do anything. On the other hand, my faith was incomplete, as long as it required a sign in order to stand firm. My faith said, "I just know that God can do this miracle; so if He proves it, I will have the faith to stand." My faith required God to do something so I could believe.

Mature, God-honoring faith is having the conviction that God is at work, even when we cannot see the evidence with our human vision. Hebrews 11:1 says, "Now faith is the assurance of things hoped for, the conviction of things not seen." If you see it, faith is no longer required. My faith was the same kind of "faith" that Thomas, Jesus' disciple, had. He said, "*If* I can see and touch the risen Lord, *then* I will believe" (John 20:25, paraphrased).

I needed the kind of faith that Abraham had. Abraham's faith said, "I am really not seeing this, Lord; but if You say so, I believe You" (Gen. 15). You may know what was said about Abraham's faith. "Abraham 'believed God, and it was counted to him as righteousness' . . . Know then that it is those of faith who are the sons of Abraham" (Gal. 3:6-7).

Conversely, Jesus said to Thomas, "Have you believed because you have seen me? Blessed are those who have not seen and yet have believed" (John 20:29). I wonder what blessing Thomas missed out on because he just wanted to trust his eyes instead of fully trusting Jesus.

I am actually glad those huge miracles did not happen for me when I asked for them as a kid. God had already done so many amazing, wonderful, and, yes, miraculous things for me that I am ashamed to have needed more proof. I'm glad to be counted among those who have not seen and yet have believed.

Sometimes, our expectations are wrong because we have a distorted image of God. Our distortion may originate in our childhood, from poor teaching, or from our own experiences. When my kids were little and I would hear a mysterious noise, my mind would go right to work to create a visual image of what could possibly be making the noise. When I smell something cooking, my nose attempts to analyze the ingredients to help me understand what I am smelling. When one of my daughters comes in late and enters my darkened room to kiss me and tell me she is home, my half-asleep mind goes to work again to imagine her expression from the sound of her voice in an attempt to evaluate if her evening has been fun or not.

The human mind is amazing—it can also be dangerous with its tendency to presume. Think of the Israelites, freshly redeemed from the land of Egypt by the mighty hand of a God they could not see. Practically the first thing they did was try to put a face to the Mighty Worker of Miracles. Of all the possibilities, they picked the face of a calf. How sad—and how grossly demeaning! Exodus 32:4-5 makes it clear that they were trying to make an image of Yahweh. But God is no calf, and He will not be cast by anyone.

Mental images we have created of God are often far from reality. Some are true but so limited that we end up worshipping a God of our own making—not very unlike the Israelites and their calf. We must learn to worship God in His entirety and accept that our human minds will never be able to take it all in.

We worship God as our loving Abba, but we must also recognize Him as uncompromisingly holy. We worship God as Redeemer, but He is also Judge. We worship God as merciful God but also as the Truth. I long to know (*yada*) the Great I AM in all His fullness, not just in the ways in which I am comfortable.

> "To whom then will you liken God, or what likeness compare with him?"
>
> Isa. 40:18

THE PITFALL OF STRIVING

Phrases we often use, like "going after God," can be tricky. It implies we should strive, an activity which comes naturally to us. But in actuality, striving is counter-productive to any relationship. For many years, I thought I was trying to get to God. He had already gotten to me! He had done all that was needed; I simply needed to spend time enjoying His Presence to deepen what He had already died to purchase for me.

Perhaps this illustration will help clarify the difference between striving and pursuing God. In the early days of my marriage to Tim, I had so many fears and insecurities, it made resting in his love nearly impossible. I was constantly asking, "Do you love me?" I was fearful he would stop loving me at some point. Others had. But fears like these hinder a close relationship. I feel his love most strongly when I am confident in his love. We strive like this in our relationship with the Lord, fearful He will stop loving us, hindering a close relationship.

Yet I still pursue my husband. Once I am confident of my husband's love, I should not stop all the myriad things I do to express my love. I must not stop pursuing a relationship with him. I pursue him from a position of knowing he loves me—not out of fear—and I continue to express my love so our relationship deepens.

Our relationship with the Lord is similar. If I pursue God simply out of fear, our intimacy will be limited; but knowing His deep love for me compels me to pursue Him all the more.

When I look back at my years of pursuing God where my life produced negligible fruit, I realize my eyes were largely on myself. I asked, *What do I need to do better? What have I done to make God silent? How can I get Him to respond?* All that introspection and striving could only take me so far. My eyes needed to turn to "the founder and perfecter of [my] faith" (Heb. 12:2) so I could see the reality: He was not distant; He was right with me. When we get our eyes off ourselves and onto our Father, we are finally able to see His perfection and let all our shortcomings fade away in His love.

When I read the account of David bringing the ark to Jerusalem (2 Sam. 6), I am struck by the number of times we are told that it was done with joy—priests rejoicing, men and women singing, David dancing. There is joy in the presence of the Lord, and joy also brings the presence of the Lord.

There are times when I revert to striving after the presence of God. I beg, and I plead. I cry and agonize, and I often get nowhere. But I have found that when I get done with my human effort to bring the Presence and just begin to thank the Lord for His presence and rejoice in the fact that He is always with me, I will invariably feel the rush of peace and joy overtake my heart and then I really do begin to sense Him with me.

Of course, David danced with all his might (2 Sam. 6:14), and that can sound like striving. But with David, it came not out of striving (which is founded in fearing you will not receive) but from a heart of gratitude and joy (which flows from trusting). Let there be joy in the presence of God!

In Ezekiel 44:17-18, Ezekiel reminds the priests that their garments are to be of linen, not wool. And then he explains that this is because they should not wear "anything that causes sweat." David also wore linen garments as he brought the ark into Jerusalem. Wearing linen speaks to the effortlessness we should have in the presence of the Lord. Remember, this is not a "religion," where man is trying by his own effort or sweat to get to God. This is a relationship in which God is reaching out to humankind.

> *"The LORD is near to all who call on him, to all who call on him in truth."*
>
> Psalm 145:18

CLOSENESS IS A CHOICE

How close would you like to be to God? How much comfort from this place of being home would you like to experience? The decision is yours. God may have different and individualized means of connecting with each person He creates, but His desire is to connect with each and every one of them. Will you be one of the ones who chooses intimacy over distance and decides that close is not close enough?

Consider Ruth: widowed, childless, and a despised foreigner. Yet she had a mother-in-law who loved her and whom she loved; and she was being cared for, protected, and provided for by wealthy relatives. She could have been comfortable with that, but Ruth wanted more. She wanted redemption, marriage, and children. She got them through determination and vulnerability. And her Boaz, a foreshadowing of our Lord Jesus, paved the way for her to become all God intended her to be through her relationship with him.

Throughout Scripture, we are shown clearly that there are blessings for those who go deeper with the Lord. From Joshua, who pursued God to greater lengths than his fellow Israelites, to the priests who consecrated themselves to draw near, we see those who pressed in for more, whose hearts could not be satisfied with anything less than companionship with God.

As we move to the New Testament, things change quite a bit in regard to companionship. Under the New Covenant, all God's children are given the choice of how close they will draw near to the Lord.

Among Jesus' disciples, we see varying levels of closeness to Jesus. Some were called by Jesus to higher levels of responsibility. In Luke 10:1, we see that seventy-two disciples were appointed for service. While they had been called out from the multitudes to serve, just as the Israelites were called out from all the peoples on earth, they were still on the periphery. The twelve disciples formed the group that was closer. They were chosen by the Lord from among the seventy-two and were privy to the times of personal teaching and training from the Lord.

But a call to responsibility does not automatically imply a closer relationship. We are not appointed to relationships; they develop reciprocally. Though the Lord wants companionship with everyone, the other half of the equation is whether we will reciprocate.

Even among the twelve, Peter, James, and John were especially close to the Lord. They are the devoted three who saw the transfiguration of Jesus. Finally, in the apostle John, we see the intimacy that truly constructed a place of companionship. Though John is called "the disciple whom Jesus loved" (John 21:20), this was not the choice of Jesus; He was not playing favorites. This was the choice of John. Just as we can, John chose how close he was going to get to Jesus. The more distant circles did not satisfy *this* seeker. John wasn't content until his head was resting on the bosom of the Lord.

For his persistence, the rewards we see in John's life are staggering. Not only did he enjoy the sweet closeness of the Lord's presence, but he also was strengthened beyond the strongest among them. No one would doubt that Peter was the disciple who was the boldest. And yet we see that while Peter was denying Jesus, John was entering into the house of the high priest, where Jesus was being tried. As Jesus was dying on the cross, John was the only disciple we see still with Him, and Jesus conferred upon him the honor and responsibility of caring for Mary, His mother.

At the resurrection, we see that John is the first of the disciples to believe that Jesus was alive. John 20:8 declares that John "saw and believed" when he went to the tomb with Peter. He was the only disciple to believe that Jesus had risen before he had seen Him. This kind of belief comes from an intimate relationship. John also had the awesome privilege of seeing Jesus—not only in His incarnation but also in His glory when Jesus appeared before John on the island of Patmos as recorded in the book of Revelation.

Within the Old Covenant, there were God-established levels that spoke of the need of a Savior to come and remove all barriers between us and God. Now, in the New Covenant, Jesus has abolished all barriers, and the choice to enter is ours. There is nothing holding us back, except our own selves. We have a choice of which level we wish our relationship with the Lord to remain. We can stay on the fringe, within the family of God, but only getting the bare minimum of God to sustain ourselves. We can go further and initiate the process of renewing our minds and sanctifying our lives. We can go even further and become of use to fellow believers by serving the Lord. Or we can choose the depths of intimacy, communion, and belonging with God that will deepen our companionship with God, changing us and changing our world.

> *"But I, through the abundance of your steadfast love, will enter your house."*
>
> Psalm 5:7a

When we endeavor to embark on this deeper relationship with our Father, we must recognize that it will not be an easy path. There are few things the enemy of our souls will oppose more than our effort to know God intimately, and there are few things with which our flesh will be less comfortable. All our beliefs and feelings must be submitted to the Lord, and what He says is the truth. We will see the fruit of our intimate moments with the Lord blossom into a rich fruit, encouraging our effort and spurring us into even deeper relationship.

> *"We destroy arguments and every lofty opinion raised against the knowledge of God, and take every thought captive to obey Christ."*
>
> 2 Cor. 10:5

CHAPTER 11
DISTRACTIONS

SOMETIMES, I THINK I HAVE conversational Attention Deficit Disorder! I am a super focused person, but my problem is that there are often just too many things to focus on—and they all want my attention right now.

My husband, Tim, comes home from work, and we sit together to talk. I tell him a bit about my day, and he tells me about his. When he is talking about people and office politics, I am right there with him. But when he begins to get technical (how many parts per trillion are in the bazillion gallon tank and how the resin reacts with the sodium hypochlorite while flowing through polyvinylidene fluoride pipes . . .), my mind leaves the conversation. I don't even realize when it leaves. One moment, I'm trying intensely to understand what Tim is saying; the next, I'm mentally preparing dinner and reviewing what we will need to do after dinner. I have taken to repeating everything Tim says when my brain is busy, so I can stay with him.

It can be even worse while I'm trying to pray and focus on the Lord. I close my eyes to pray and listen, but my to-do list is knocking on my brain. Without realizing it, my eyes drift open and I'm staring out the window. "Those bushes need pruning . . . Isn't that gerbera daisy blossoming beautifully? I better water it . . . I wonder how many oranges we'll get this year. I wonder if they'll be as icky as they were last year . . . I need to ask Tim to kill those ants that are digging out all the sand from the pavers . . . Poor Tim, he has so much on his plate right now . . . How can we find more time? . . . Oh, Lord, help Tim . . . OH

YEAH, I WAS PRAYING!" I slam my eyes shut in an attempt to focus and begin to pray again, only now, I am more than a little irritated with myself.

I know it is not the Lord's fault. He is not a bore (not that Tim is either). There is no more thrilling time of my day than when I finally quiet down this brain and hear Him. It is always a work in progress, though.

Our flesh is easily distracted and longs to be entertained more than it desires to focus. The Lord bemoans the lack of attention span and fading commitment of Israel when He says, "'What shall I do with you, O Ephraim? What shall I do with you, O Judah? Your love is like a morning cloud, like the dew that goes early away'" (Hosea 6:4).

It is difficult to keep our minds occupied with the business of Heaven when the business of earth so readily consumes our senses. We all live with a mind that wanders and needs to be brought into subjection.

Although we frequently attribute our inability to focus on our modern era of entertainment, instant gratification, and over-stimulation, Brother Lawrence, the seventeenth century monk who wrote that book of my grandma's that fell into my lap, showed that this is a human condition we must all work to overcome.

> Our mind is extremely roving . . . When the mind . . . has contracted certain bad habits of wandering and dissipation, they are difficult to overcome, and commonly draw us, even against our wills, to the things of the earth . . . Let it be your business to keep your mind in the presence of the Lord. If it sometimes wander and withdraw itself from Him, do not much disquiet yourself for that: trouble and disquiet serve rather to distract the mind than to recollect it; the will must bring it back in tranquility. If you persevere in this manner, God will have pity on you. One way to recollect the mind easily in the time of prayer, and preserve it more in tranquility, is *not to let it wander too far at other times.* You should keep it strictly in the presence of God; and being accustomed to think of Him often, you will

find it easy to keep your mind calm in the time of prayer, or at least to recall it from its wanderings.[12]

These distractions are often the "cares of this world" referred to by Jesus in the parable of the sower (Matt. 13), and they will choke out whatever the Lord wishes to grow in us if we do not learn to choose to press past them and press into the presence of God. This is not something that is done once and for all time. This is a continual exercise. Just as with physical exercise, it can never be considered complete, as left to itself, our ability to press past distraction will atrophy as readily as the human body. But as we do it consistently and repeatedly, we will gain strength in this area.

JESUS TAUGHT US HOW

Jesus teaching His disciples to pray in Matthew 6:6 is profoundly instructive for developing the habit of the secret place, a place of quiet where we can meet with God. He says, "But when you pray, go into your room and shut the door and pray to your Father who is in secret. And your Father who sees in secret will reward you." In this we can see three instructions and a helpful reminder to our flesh.

The first instruction is that we need to find a place to be alone. Even in the busiest of places, we can find a place to be alone because the secret place we are called to enter is not a physical location. Although it will be easier for our minds to focus in a place where we are entirely alone (particularly in the beginning), we need to get alone with God in our spirits in order to commune with Him. Finding that quiet place in your spirit is crucial to having an intimate time with the Lord.

Sometimes, it can be difficult to find that spiritual secret place. Even our language implies a physical place. It would make it so much easier if it were!

---

12 Brother Lawrence, *The Practice of the Presence of God* (Westwood: Fleming H. Revell, 1958), 51.

However, it is a spiritual place, a place of peace where you have a knowing in your spirit that you are aware of the attention of God and He has your full attention. Although it gets easier with practice to "find" this place, initially it can be difficult.

The Lord knows our flesh and the difficulties we have in this area, so His second instruction follows. He reminds us that we must shut the door. This involves closing out any distraction our flesh or the enemy brings to our minds. We must close the door to everything to maintain this exclusive time with the Lord. We must even shut out the requests we wish to lay before the Lord. When you are having intimate time with your spouse, you do not wish to hear a to-do list. Your goal is simply to enjoy your time together without worrying about the "outside world." The same is true in our time with the Lord. There will be a time for presenting our requests to Him; but when we are endeavoring to speak to and hear Him on an intimate level, we need to shut everything else out.

In order to quiet the mind to focus on the Lord, some people get physically hushed, while others pray in the Spirit until the input from the outside world is silenced. Some worship. Some get emotionally or mentally quiet, while others place a picture in their minds of the Lord's throne room or Him sitting with them in order to help their minds focus. Bear in mind that we do not *empty* our minds as is done in Eastern meditation or yoga. We are, instead, *focusing* our minds on the Lord, His goodness, His Word, and His promises.

If you are in a season where you are particularly distracted, you may find that keeping a notepad beside you to jot down thoughts that come to mind will help you. I have found this helpful from time to time. It is hard to focus in and hear from the Lord when you are mentally trying not to forget that you need to do various tasks that you only seem to remember when you are trying to listen! Go ahead and write them down and get back to focusing on the Lord.

Third, we pray. Jesus told us to go into our secret place, to close the door, and then to pray. We speak to the Father and allow Him to speak to us. We tell Him of our love for Him, and He communicates His love to us. We are not in charge of the conversation; He is. There may be times when He speaks to us about things that need to change in us, or He directs us with practical wisdom. Ask Him questions and listen for the Holy Spirit to answer. It is an opportunity to grow deeper in our relationship by listening and obeying and just soaking in His glorious presence.

There are two essentials that I recommend you have at the ready as you take time in the secret place—your Bible and a journal. One of the primary ways the Lord speaks to us is through His written Word, what the Greek calls *logos*. God's Word is living and active (Heb. 4:12). That means it has the capability to speak to us and guide us as the Holy Spirit directs us where He wants us to read. Slow down as you read and reflect on what the Lord is speaking to you through the passage He has led you to.

I also find it vital to keep my journal handy. When the Lord begins to speak, you will want to make note of what He is saying to you. What God speaks to you in these moments and what He makes come alive to you in His written Word are called *rhema* in the Greek. *Rhema* indicates a word from the Lord that becomes a sword in our hand with which we can beat back the enemy (Eph. 6:17).

Writing out what I feel the Lord is speaking is an act of reverence to God. Like most people, I struggle with remembering in detail the things I have heard; and when the most important Person of all is speaking, I want to remember every syllable! I grab for my journal and a pencil and sometimes write a phrase, a sentence, or a full-fledged download. We cannot expect to grow if we are not obedient to the word of the Lord, and we cannot expect to be obedient if we don't remember what we have heard. I know that I have heard things that so touched my heart that I felt sure I would remember them later, only to find that I can only remember the gist of them at best. I honor the word of the Lord when I take the trouble to write it down.

Also, by writing things down, I can test them. If I go back over what I have written and it does not line up with the Word of God in the Bible, I need to throw it out. We are instructed to test our own words and the words of others (1 Thess. 5:19-21; 1 John 4:1-3). Writing things down and being willing to submit it to the written Word's scrutiny is another way to honor the Lord.

I cannot adequately express the joy that comes from being able to refer back in my journals to previous instructions or encouragements from the Lord. The words God has spoken to me in the past get sweeter to me with each passing year and propel me forward with faith.

After these three instructions on how to pray, Jesus offers us a practical reminder. The Father is unseen. This is an excellent clue for our flesh. There may be times of goosebumps and rapturous joy, but we cannot rely on those fleshly clues for detecting the presence of God. Our Father is omnipresent; He is everywhere at all times. Often, we must exercise our faith in His Presence, even when we do not feel it in our physical bodies. The more mature in the Lord you become, the more you may find this a reality; for more is expected of the mature. In moments like these, simply begin thanking the Lord for His Presence in faith and allow peace to begin to fill your heart.

Bear in mind that all of this instruction in prayer (and even the Lord's Prayer found in Matthew 6:9-13) are all founded in the context of relationship. Notice how Jesus repeatedly emphasizes that we are to pray to our Father. All prayer must come from a foundation of intimate relationship. It is in knowing your place as a child of God that the magnitude of acceptance will come alive to you. It is from the vantage point of being His that you develop unshakable faith and experience that intimate relationship for which your heart longs. It is here that you finally get a taste of the depths of longing the Father has for you, His child.

Coming to know God as Father may be difficult for some, but it is important. God is your loving, caring, nurturing Father. If this is a concept that is uncomfortable or even painful for you, I encourage you to not sweep it away but to deal with the causes behind the pain so that you can embrace your gracious Heavenly Father. There is healing in coming to know His perfect love toward you.

TIPS

These are some of my favorite tips for focusing in the secret place:

First, invite the Holy Spirit and uninvite the enemy! Go ahead, tell the enemy to keep quiet. You have the authority in the name of Jesus.

Start with praise and thanksgiving. Focusing on the greatness of my God helps drown out all the clatter of my worries.

Pray out loud. This helps me focus while I'm praying; but of course, you cannot hear Him if you are the only one talking. So, this only works for part of prayer—the part that involves talking, not listening.

Journal. This is another tool to help focus our minds and remember what the Lord has spoken. When you journal, pour out your heart to God, but don't forget to also write down what you hear Him saying as your heart gets quiet before Him.

Recognize where you are. You are not just in your prayer closet; you are at the Throne of God! If I acknowledge and see myself there, my focus is not only better, it is also heightened.

Our desire and our ability to control our minds may vary; however, God's desire is unfading. He desires us when we desire Him with intensity, though He knows our intensity will wane. He is always waiting and desiring our devotion. His love will never falter or waver. And if we detect within our spirits a longing for intimacy with God, we can trust that the Author of that longing gave it to us and has an even more intense longing for us. He will fulfill the longing. He knows that though our devotion fades like a mist (Hosea 6:4), He promises to be faithful.

> *"One thing have I asked of the LORD, that will I seek after: that I may dwell in the house of the LORD all the days of my life, to gaze upon the beauty of the LORD and to inquire in his temple."*
>
> Psalm 27:4

CHAPTER 12
PREPARE YOUR HEART

FALLING IN LOVE IS EXCITING! It is full of the thrill of the pursuit and the thrill of being pursued. Love can consume our thoughts in the early days as we reflect on our recent moments together and anticipate the next moments that will come. Those days are full of stomach-tumbling, finger-tingling excitement.

When love has come to stay, when commitment is the next step, some shy away and turn apathetic. The same can be true in our love relationship with the Lord. The excitement we feel at the initial phases of this relationship may ebb and flow, but true love pursues commitment and makes whatever efforts are required to fully express love.

The woman in the Song of Songs experienced this. When her lover came calling, she was unwilling to put forth the effort. "I slept, but my heart was awake. A sound! My beloved is knocking. 'Open to me, my sister, my love, my dove, my perfect one, for my head is wet with dew, my locks with the drops of the night.' I had put off my garment; how could I put it on? I had bathed my feet; how could I soil them?" (Song of Songs 5:2-3).

Too often the distractions of this world come to limit the relationship we have with the Lord. Effort and time are required for any relationship, and the same is true of our relationship with the Father. We must be willing to put forth the effort required, to withstand every opposition, to rise to the challenge of every obstacle—to soil our feet—in order to greet our Love with a willing heart.

In the parable of the sower, we see that there are several reasons why the seed that God tries to implant does not always produce the intended fruit.

> The sower sows the word. And these are the ones along the path, where the word is sown: when they hear, Satan immediately comes and takes away the word that is sown in them. And these are the ones sown on rocky ground: the ones who, when they hear the word, immediately receive it with joy. And they have no root in themselves, but endure for a while; then, when tribulation or persecution arises on account of the word, immediately they fall away. And others are the ones sown among thorns. They are those who hear the word, but the cares of the world and the deceitfulness of riches and the desires for other things enter in and choke the word, and it proves unfruitful. But those that were sown on the good soil are the ones who hear the word and accept it and bear fruit, thirtyfold and sixtyfold and a hundredfold (Mark 4:14-20).

We all want our seed to produce abundantly. We all want that bumper crop of thirty, sixty, or a hundredfold. But be honest, not every seed we allow to be planted has this kind of yield. And the fault is not in the seed, which is God's Word. The best place to start to discern why our yield may be low is written right there in this parable. Let's examine the reasons Jesus has given for our less-than-abundant crop production.

GOD'S SEED ON THE PATH

Perhaps our ground, our heart, is unwilling or unready to receive the Word; and it remains hardened like a path, unable to take in any good the Lord tries to plant. We will be easy prey to the enemy, who is always desiring to be our thief. As a woman past the age of childbearing whose ovaries cannot produce eggs and whose womb is no longer able to provide a place for seed to grow, the seed may come; but it will find nothing to unite itself to, no place to implant and grow.

It is time to do a grounds inspection. Honestly evaluate your willingness to walk this road. This is more than a dating relationship. Are you one who wants to flirt but never wants to marry? Perhaps you really love the fun; but when commitment and responsibility are called for, you are unable to cope. So often, we appreciate the goosebumps of worship and encounters with God but shy away from the daily sacrifice it takes to make a relationship work. Sometimes, we just want a place to belong and feel at home without anyone telling us the truth about ourselves. Be willing to soften your ground to make it hospitable to seeds. Be willing to be a place where God can let His dreams for you grow.

If your ground has grown hard with time, you may need to make the effort to soften it again. As new gardens often need to be re-tilled each year, perhaps you need to re-till the soil of your heart. Do not allow anything that does not belong in your garden to have access to it, lest the foot traffic cause your heart to revert to a hardened path.

Perhaps time has caused a hardening. My husband asked me to marry him on the balcony of a restaurant in our hometown. It was a beautiful, starlit, April night. In the center of a platter of desserts our waiter was tempting us with, was a small, gray box with a red satin bow. He asked what I would choose from the platter. Naturally, I requested the mystery box!

Unfortunately, the restaurant has since closed; but we have repeatedly sat in our car, staring up at that balcony, reminiscing. We were so young. We were so in love. We were so excited about what God was doing with us. Reminiscing does something for you. Not only is it fun, but it also stirs up those initial feelings of love and affection you first had. Revisiting why you love each other can restore love when you are feeling tired, bored, or indifferent.

To bask in God's love and reminisce over those first realizations of His passion for you and your passion for Him revitalizes that feeling. Conversely, we become numb and hardened when we take our relationship with the Lord for granted.

Like the Shulamite woman in the Song of Songs, I can spark and rekindle my love and passion for the Lord by meditating on what makes Him so wonderful. In Song of Songs 5:10-16, the beloved goes into great detail to recount the splendors of her lover, describing him from head to toe with love and adoration. If we spent more time proclaiming our love and adoration for our Lord, it would be like a till for the hardened places in us.

Perhaps neglect has caused a hardening. My husband and I have actually had the odd experience late in the summers here in Arizona of our swimming pool getting too warm. Without any mechanism to heat it except the sun, it has gotten so warm, it is no longer refreshing. When the kids were little, we had races on blocks of ice just to make the tepid pool fun again! We must closely watch the pool to make sure it does not become a breeding ground for algae.

I wonder how often I am spiritually growing algae because I have allowed my heart to grow lukewarm and indifferent. I wonder how often I have lost touch with the fire of God without even realizing I am the one who has let go. Like being spiritually pick-pocketed, I have grown so ambivalent toward what is so sacred that I am bereft of it without even noticing.

I'm not trying to beat up on myself. I know we all go through times when we have difficulty kicking ourselves into gear. C.S. Lewis calls this "undulation." It is normal to have times when burn-out or fatigue tries to cripple our forward motion and make us doubt our sincerity. But what I'm concerned about is a time that may start with undulation but becomes chronic. It becomes a way of life. These are the times when we must fight back.

This was the problem in the Laodicean church of Revelation 3:14-16. The hot springs of Hierapolis to the north of them were thought to have wonderful healing properties. People would flock to them in hope of finding relief from every manner of pain. The cold springs of Colossae to the south were known to be a source of refreshment. Weary travelers went out of their way to experience them. But Laodicea was stuck in the middle, notorious for its lack of adequate water, not offering the world a drink of anything that would be truly beneficial.

No one wants a drink of lukewarm water from a stagnant pond. We need to be either hot waters of healing or cold waters of refreshing, and the way to be that is to be near the Source. Jesus, speaking to the Laodicean church, gives them this cure, if they are willing. He says, "'Behold, I stand at the door and knock. If anyone hears my voice and opens the door, I will come in to him and eat with him, and he with me'" (Rev. 3:20).

Getting in close communion with our Lord, our Source, is the only remedy for the hopeless stagnation and ineffectiveness into which we may have slipped. We must have this time with the Lord flowing into us if we are going to have anything worth giving to those around us.

Perhaps insensitivity to the Spirit has caused a hardening. I have a pet peeve. As with most of my irritations, it centers on traffic. There is a freeway where I live that has a frontage road alongside it. Wherever there are exit ramps onto the frontage road, the frontage traffic is *supposed* to yield to the ramp traffic. They do not. They do not even slow down. I don't think they even look! I like justice and have to work to resist the urge to teach them a lesson by running them over or at least shaking my fist at them.

After nearly being run over by yet another unyielding driver recently, I got to thinking about how we need to yield to the Holy Spirit. But practically speaking, what does that look like? So often, His leading is so subtle, and we often miss it altogether.

Yielding does not always require us to come to a full stop. Often, we just need to alter our speed. This is so true with the Holy Spirit. As He leads and guides me throughout the day, He is not usually requiring me to make a complete alteration to my course, just a reordering of my priorities. Who is in charge—the Holy Spirit or me? Whose time is it, anyway—His or mine?

Yielding means allowing the Holy Spirit to come first and putting our needs and desires in submission to Him. When I hear that still, small Voice wooing me and asking me to drop everything and spend time with Him, I need to be willing to yield.

I am concerned with my propensity to be in such a hurry that I never hear the Spirit calling me to yield at all. Just like those people on the frontage road, I can be so focused on where I'm headed that I never even notice Him trying to enter in front of me and lead the way. This calls for a decision and discipline to be listening, continually aware of His presence and willing to sense His direction. If I'm not listening for Him, I may never even know that I have run Him off the road.

GOD'S SEED IN THE STONY GROUND

If the ground of your heart is rocky, the seed will not find a home for long. Trials and tribulations will cause it to die. As Jesus says in the parable, they received the word with joy, but reality caused it to wilt. These people choose to abort the life that was beginning to grow within them. The commitment has been made in theory; but when the actual task of following God becomes a reality, they opt out and kill what God has implanted in their heart. The realities of a new life can cause more pain than the initial excitement and joy of promise led you to believe. And sometimes, my comfort-loving self can think, *This can't be God. It doesn't feel good!*

How do you cope amid the trials of life? Personally, I think I do admirably with the monumental mountains of difficulty that appear in my path. I know where to turn, and I hang onto my faith with tenacity. I go into the crisis armed for battle and ready for what is coming. However, I have seen far too often, it is the medium-sized boulders of life with which I have difficulty—the lingering head cold that moves into a sinus infection, the anticipated bonus that must pay for new tires instead of the getaway, or the family member who made me feel small. For some reason, it seems that those are the ones that catch me off guard. I get disillusioned by them as if I thought they should be foreign to my life. In the scheme of things, those medium-sized rocks will not matter when I am on my deathbed; but somehow, they are the ones that have the capability to make my joy fade, cause me to wilt, and make me fruitless. I stand, withering in the heat, calling my core beliefs into question, and threatening the life of my seed.

I'm sure you have had times, like I have, where you feel as though the wind has totally been knocked out of you, when you are not even sure you can continue to put one foot in front of the other, and when you are not even sure how you will get out of bed the next morning.

When Jesus was born into this world, He entered a culture that was expecting Him. They knew He was coming; but when He arrived, He was far from what they had expected. Great debate raged among the Jews of the time. Would Messiah come as a Second Adam to restore the garden? Would He come as the Second Moses and bring a new exodus from oppression? Would He come as the Second David and reestablish the kingdom of Israel? Though Jesus came as all of these, He did it in spiritual ways that the Jews were not expecting. They wanted tangibles (and really, who could blame them?).

Everything He did disappointed them. He spoke of peace and communion with God, but they wanted the real Garden of Eden. He delivered thousands from Satan and fed over five thousand with next to nothing, but they wanted to be delivered to the ultimate Promised Land and see manna fall. He came to establish the Kingdom of Heaven, but they wanted Israel to once again become a world power and overthrow Rome. They were bitterly disillusioned.

But disillusionment is not an end; it is the crossroads at which a life-altering decision is before you. Fall away or stand. John 6:66 tells us that many disciples of Jesus turned back from following Him because of this disillusionment. Yet so precious to me are the resigned words of Peter, himself disillusioned: "'Lord, to whom shall we go? You have the words of eternal life, and we have believed, and have come to know, that you are the Holy One of God'" (John 6:68-69).

I don't know about you, but I have been there in that "dark night of the soul" when utter devastation blots out even the faintest glimmer of hope. All that you thought was foundational gives way, and you don't feel there is anything on which to hold. But to whom shall you go? Then, though it is not always as you had hoped or expected, as you choose to stand firm in the darkness, a hand reaches out to you.

It is the tree that grows in buffeting winds that is well-rooted. Instead of giving in to the storm, it has sent its roots deeper. A tree doesn't wildly flail its branches, trying to find another tree to grasp onto for stability, nor does it put its hope in its own strength—the mightiest of trees has fallen and revealed its lack of roots. A tree finds its security in strengthening its hold on what it knows will not shift or change. Sending your roots deeper into God will be the only thing that brings you through a storm. Run to Him, in spite of feeling disillusioned. God will hold you close as your heart breaks.

Let go of those stones that are trying to choke you out and instead root your heart in the heart of God.

GOD'S SEED IN THORNY GROUND

The thorny ground spoken of in the parable speaks of misplaced priorities. We are unwilling to lay all else in this world aside to let God's claim on our hearts stand, firmly rooted in our commitment to follow Him. His call to us does not rank first in our lives.

You are entering an undivorceable marriage. Are you willing to be "the real you" with Him? Sometimes even harder and scarier: are you willing to let God be Himself? Are you willing to accept all aspects of Him, not just the ones you find comfortable and nice? As C.S. Lewis put it so aptly, "He is not safe, but He is good."[13]

Have you noticed how you can almost always tell when you are driving behind someone who is talking on their cell phone? It's irritating. More than irritating, it's downright dangerous! They are all over the place and do not even know it. In fact, I have driven with a couple of people who I would consider excellent and skillful drivers—until they answer their phones. Suddenly, they do not know where to turn; their speed varies; and they are unaware of the fact that they are now straddling lanes! There is no hand available to turn on the blinker, so that goes out the window, along with reaction times and peripheral vision.

The scariest aspect of this is that they are completely oblivious to their sudden ineptness. They think they are just as capable on the phone as off. They are clueless to the fact that they look like they deserve a blinking bumper sticker that screams, "STUDENT DRIVER!"

It makes me wonder how many of us drive through life like this, splitting our focus between so many things that we are really focused on nothing at all. We start off headed in the right direction but then lose our focus and wander through the maze of life without any priority at all.

Each of us needs to decide what our life's focus is going to be and pursue it with singleness of heart. That does not mean that I don't do anything but that one thing; but it means that in everything I am called upon to do, my priority shines through. If my singular focus is to pursue an intimate relationship with God, that is my destination. Whether I'm cleaning the house, caring for a friend, raising my children, or loving my husband, my pursuit of God is central and seen in all I do. I would choose to do things in an excellent way and for His glory.

This may mean that some things are cut out of my life—things I may have enjoyed but would take me in a different direction than my one pursuit.

---

13 C.S. Lewis, *The Lion, the Witch and the Wardrobe* (New York: Collier, 1976), 76.

Cutting things out may seem painful, but it would be much more painful to reach my life's end and realize I had never made it to my destination. I am not saying we should never give ourselves time to have rest, relaxation, and recreation. Our gracious Lord made this world for us to enjoy, and rest is part of being able to do our best at our primary focus.

Nevertheless, there are pressures to do everything in an effort to "have it all." And there are fleshly pressures that pull us away from what is of paramount importance. When our daily time of listening to the Lord's voice is continually put to the side as we pursue our own agendas, we need to learn to let the things of this world be what fall to the wayside. We need to establish the central things that make up our primary focus and build our lives around them, instead of letting our lives squeeze out what is most essential to the core of our existence. We need to know where we are going and not let anything deter us. We need to hang up and drive!

"Be still before the LORD and wait patiently for him."

Psalm 37:7a

PART 4
A PRACTICAL PATH

CHAPTER 13
MILE MARKERS ON YOUR PATH

THERE WAS A LOW CHATTER of friendly fellowship as I turned a folding chair to face him. Tim, my husband, did the same. We were out-of-town guests, and this felt like our chance to get this burning question answered without the shame that had come to accompany this subject for us. I had been probing, listening, and reading everywhere I could, to no avail.

I wanted to hear from God myself—not just subsist on second-hand manna someone else had received from the Lord. I wanted the comfort of my Good Shepherd's voice as He had promised in John 10.

I was embarrassed that I did not already know what seemed to be second nature to most of the people around us. "Hearing from God" had quickly turned into just another area where rejection greeted me with her nasty curled lip and up and down glances, shut the door on the party, and refused me entry. Yet for all my fear of my appearance of not being in the "in" crowd at the "hearing from God" party, I was not above crawling through a window.

And that is what gave me the rare courage to speak out to this stranger, the pastor sitting before me like a guru on a mountain top, ready with his sage advice. My questions and frustrations all came tumbling out. I had been trying so hard and for so long to hear God's voice. I had thought I had heard several times; but a few of those times, I had been horribly wrong.

"How do you hear from God?" I asked and then held my breath, waiting for him to lay before me the key I had been searching for and missing.

"Well," he boomed, "I'd just insist on it!"

Insist on it? Did I hear that right? Images of an arm-wrestling match with the Creator of the universe flashed to mind as I tried to wrap my head around his words. I was to do what, exactly? Hunger strike? Throw a tantrum before the Throne of Glory until God uttered words from His lips? Sit before Him silently until delirium took over?

Where frustration and embarrassment had been, anger began to boil. I wanted to yell and call the man an idiot. I managed a weak "okay" before thanking him for his time, silently bundling our little children in the car with Tim and driving away in tears.

WHAT WE'VE LEARNED SO FAR

Once I really got a handle on hearing from the Lord, it became a passion to help others, to not allow the smugness of those I had humbly queried to settle in on me, too. I truly want to help you know the Lord's voice, not just wax on about how wonderful it is.

It is time to get practical. But first, let's review some of what we have already learned.

1. All of us need this. It is not only for the weak or for those who cannot find the way by their own reason. We need the voice of God as a mark of our identity as sons and daughters.
2. God desires this. He does not give companionship grudgingly. His desire for companionship far outstrips your desire for Him. And He has provided a way for us to have that relationship in Jesus Christ. We can recapture the beauty of fellowship Adam and Eve had with the Lord in the garden.

3. When we speak of "companionship," we are speaking of knowing someone at the deepest level possible. We will not be satisfied with anything superficial. After all, Jesus taught that the real way to the Father was through intimate relationship.
4. In the Old Testament, a select few "walked with God," but now that type of companionship is available to all believers in Jesus Christ.
5. There are countless benefits to this type of relationship. We are strengthened in our inner being as we are rooted in this love relationship and are blessed with peace and a heavenly perspective. We are also blessed with the Holy Spirit leading and guiding us and blessing our lives with joy and transforming us into Christ's image.
6. What a blessing to finally find ourselves in a reality in which we are thoroughly known and thoroughly loved. It is a joy to our hearts as well as a blessing to those around us as we become the light of the world we were designed to be.
7. We have learned to let all feelings of unworthiness fall away. We know those insecurities are really lies of the enemy to keep us distant from our Good Shepherd. God loves us!
8. We are also rejecting all lies that keep us in a willful place of distance from the Lord. We will not be fooled by lies that make us fear that God will overwhelm our lives. We will not put too much stock in our feelings, thinking that if we are not feeling Him, God is not there. We rely on faith and want the real deal, not just what appears good.
9. We acknowledge that we have a choice in all this. We know that striving is futile and counter-productive, but we also recognize that whatever level of closeness we desire is the one that we will pursue.
10. We have learned from Jesus' wise instruction that we can shut the door on distractions so we can hear the Father.

"HEARING" FROM GOD

When we talk about hearing from God, it is easy to get confused about exactly what we mean. Do we mean literal "hearing"? "Hearing from God," though a common and apt phrase, can also be a bit of a misnomer. People infrequently hear God speak with their actual ears. In fact, there are four common ways people "hear" from God.

Of these four ways, you may be more comfortable with one than the others, but I would caution you against claiming any single avenue as the way God speaks to you. God is not One for being put in a box. Let God speak to you in any manner He chooses. He may speak to you for years in one way and then switch. He may speak to you in all these ways in the span of one day. Just as we communicate to one another in various ways, the Lord also speaks in a variety of ways.

These four ways seem to be the most common:

1. **Hearing**. Yes, there are times when people hear God. Though it is rarely audible, they hear Him most often in their spirits—God's Spirit communicating directly to their spirit. It can sound quite a bit like your own voice in your head but is much wiser and more virtuous than what you normally say to yourself. It will be kinder, more compassionate, and humbler than your natural internal self. The voice of the Spirit will often drop a thought into your mind that would never have crossed your mind before, like, "Go pray for that co-worker," or "I'm with you to help you."
2. **Seeing**. Just as "hearing" rarely involves your literal ears, "seeing" rarely involves your literal eyes. And in much the same way as it is with "hearing," seeing from the Lord in your mind will surprise you with wisdom and virtue that is beyond your own wisdom and virtue. With my eyes closed, I have seen Scripture references

in my mind or a broken heart in a friend I'm praying for mended by the Lord. There are times I see just a single image, and the Lord speaks a message from that one image. There are other times a full scene plays out on the screen of my mind.

3. **Knowing**. This is an otherwise inexplicable confidence in an impression from the Lord. You will suddenly know something that is outside your natural knowledge. Perhaps it is fleeting; but other times, it will not leave you alone and is persistent. Some have described this as "knowing in your knower," and that seems to be an apt description. This may be what Paul describes as an "utterance of knowledge" (1 Cor. 12:8) and may happen as you pray for someone and suddenly know something that you have never been told. It can happen when you are seeking the Lord for direction, and you suddenly and inexplicably have a peaceful knowing that tells you which road to take.

4. **Feeling**. This can be either a feeling in your body or in your soul. You could get a sensation in your body that communicates something to you or be overwhelmed with a feeling in your soul that communicates from the Lord. You may feel overwhelming compassion for someone who needs prayer. Feelings can come through other senses, too. Once I suddenly smelled something nostalgic from my childhood without any natural source, but I knew exactly what the Lord was communicating to me through it.

Regardless of how the Lord communicates with you, be open to what He is saying while always checking it against what the Word of God says about the subject and about the character of God. If it does not line up with the Word, do not get overly concerned; and by all means, do not give up on listening to God. Simply throw it out and start again. Remember, hearing from God is something that must be exercised. It is not an instant download; it is companionship that must be built and trained over time and with practice.

> *"Make me to know your ways, O LORD; teach me your paths.*
> *Lead me in your truth and teach me, for you are the God of my salvation;*
> *for you I wait all the day long."*
>
> Psalm 25:4-5

CHAPTER 14
HOW COMPANIONSHIP IS ATTAINED

THERE ARE NO CAST-IN-STONE STEPS to finding this place of intimacy with God. God deals with each of us on an individual basis, and it is never the same for two people. It is pointless to try to make it something formulaic. In our humanness, we often wish for clear-cut, concrete steps to our spiritual destination. But spiritual journeys take place in the realm of the spirit; there are no mathematical formulas where I can simply add two and two and arrive at my answer.

I can only testify to what God has done with me and what I have seen Him do in those who are close to me. God is Sovereign, and the only thing that is predictable is that He is unpredictable. If in His sovereignty, He chooses to bypass things He has brought me through, I am quite sure that the character developed in the process I have seen will be developed in His own ways and timing. God does not have a cookie cutter curriculum for each of His children. He treats us according to our needs.

The process is important. It would be the worst shame of all to attain something and then lose it because of a lack of character that the process would have produced. "Process" is far from exciting. It is often boring and, at times, even painful. But it is the means that God often uses to bring us to maturity. My exhortation to you is to be desirous enough of an intimate relationship with God to go through the process. Whatever it may cost you will be worth it.

While there is no step-by-step process in the development of an intimate relationship with God, there is one rather obvious prerequisite and some attributes that will help a person to come to a deeper relationship with the Lord.

God is the Creator of cause and effect, and we cannot claim that grace covers over our unwillingness to commit to Him with wholeheartedness any more than we can claim that grace cancels out the law of gravity. God *is* gracious and forgiving when we fail to pursue the attributes that follow, but we cannot treat God as a Codependent Who is willing to overlook issues just to maintain peace. He is willing to accept baby believers where they are and love them every step of the way, but He will bring each of us into maturity.

THE PREREQUISITE: SALVATION

Anyone who desires this relationship with the Lord must be His child. Coming into the family of God is required of all who wish to have an intimate relationship with God. Though being saved is a prerequisite, it is simple to meet. Renounce your sins, trusting that Jesus took them upon Himself. "Confess . . . with your mouth that Jesus is Lord and believe in your heart that God raised him from the dead" (Rom. 10:9). This is how each of us are saved and from where we embark on our intimate relationship with the Lord.

Salvation can be seen as a transaction. It is an exchange. We are asking God to take all of our mess and give us His perfection. What an unfair exchange! But our Abba deeply desires to make it—in fact, He died to be able to make it! He brings each of us to the point of realizing that we cannot make it on our own; we cannot be perfect on our own; and we cannot attain Heaven or peace with Him on our own. That is when He steps in and reveals that we don't have to. He wants to do it for us. He wants to *be* our Salvation, not just provide it. He wants to be the only One we rely on, not our own "good" works or willpower to do the right things.

We are saved simply by acknowledging our dependence on Him for our salvation and asking Him to accept Jesus' sacrifice of His life instead of the punishment we ought to have for our participation in the great rebellion against Him. It is by this faith that Jesus' sacrificial death can be accepted as our substitute, thereby saving us. Romans 5:1 and 10 say, "Therefore, since we have been justified by faith, we have peace with God through our Lord Jesus Christ . . . For if while we were enemies we were reconciled to God by the death of his Son, much more, now that we are reconciled, shall we be saved by his life."

Are you wondering how to be saved? Accept the free gift that God has extended to each and every human being. As if reaching out to accept a gift from a friend or as easy as taking the hand of someone who loves you, so is receiving salvation easy. There are three basic parts of salvation:

1. **Confess Who God is.** "Lord, I know you are God. I know You created me. You chose to become a human being Yourself to show me that you love me. I know that You came and died for me to make me acceptable in Your sight. I believe that Jesus rose from the dead as proof that His sacrifice was the acceptable sacrifice in my place."

2. **Confess who you are.** "Lord, I know that I am not worthy to be counted as Your child. I know that the things I have done and thought make me imperfect and are sin."

3. **Make the exchange.** "Lord, I thank You that You came to exchange my sin for Your holiness and perfection. Right now, I accept that exchange. I ask You to take all my sins and nail them to the cross and make me holy in Your sight. I ask You to take all my pain and give me Your joy. I ask You to take my brokenness

and give me the wholeness You have for me. I ask You to take my old ways of thinking and help me to renew my mind so that I think like You. I ask You to take my old ways of living and help me to live for You and like You would. I give You all my life, and I accept the wonderful life You have prepared for me.

"I thank You, Jesus, for dying for my sins. I thank You that You love me and want me to be Your child. I love You and accept You as my Savior and my God. Please help me to get to know You deeply and to follow You all my life. Thank You, Lord, for Your graciousness to me. In Jesus name, Amen."

Yes, it is that easy. You just made the best exchange of your life! Now, get into a church where you can grow in your knowledge of God. He so heartily wants you to know Him. Read His Word, the Bible, and talk to Him and listen for His voice with your heart.

> *"If you confess with your mouth that Jesus is Lord and believe in your heart that God raised him from the dead, you will be saved."*
>
> Rom. 10:9

FAITH

Faith is an absolute necessity in one's relationship with God. Hebrews 11:6 makes it clear that unless we have faith, we will not be rewarded with the satisfaction of having the relationship with God we seek: "Without faith it is impossible to please him, for whoever would draw near to God must believe that he exists and that he rewards those who seek him." In fact, we are told that it is only "with a true heart in full assurance of faith" that we are able to "draw near" to God (Heb. 10:22).

In Ephesians, Paul prays for the believers "that according to the riches of his glory [God] may grant you to be strengthened with power through his Spirit in your inner being, so that Christ may dwell in your hearts through faith" (Eph. 3:16-17). To "dwell" means to live in, to make your home in. This is what we want from the Lord—to make His home in our hearts, to be Immanuel, "God with us," to be with us in intimate companionship. And the Lord dwells in our hearts through faith (v. 17).

It is only through faith that we are able to conceive of God desiring to have fellowship with us, and we must maintain this faith through the onslaught of doubt that would assail us if we endeavor to make our way to the heart of God.

The book of Hebrews calls "an unbelieving" heart an "evil" heart (Heb. 3:12). We must guard against it. We must never attempt to excuse it by thinking it is merely a humble heart that sees itself as so small and God as so great as to make the chasm too vast. We must line up our thinking with the Word of God and stand in faith that what Jesus Christ accomplished for us is indeed accomplished. Our faith should not be—indeed, it *could* not be—based on ourselves, our merit, or our ability to enter into His presence. Our faith must be based in one thing alone: the work of Jesus Christ.

> *"In [Christ Jesus] we have boldness and access with confidence through our faith in him."*
>
> Eph. 3:12

REPENTANCE

Beyond the need for faith, the gateway to intimacy with God is repentance. Without faith, one would not even bother to approach the Lord. But it is only with a repentant heart that we can ever step past the doorway into His presence. Repentance sets our hearts in right relation with God. Though we must come with boldness, our boldness is based on the blood of Jesus, not our merit. Repentance is how we acknowledge our utter bankruptcy and need for a Savior Who has paid the price.

Our flesh has no place in the holy presence of God, and we must strip ourselves of our flesh before we may enter. This is what the Word of God often refers to as having a circumcised heart (Deut. 10:16, 30:6; Jer. 4:4; Rom. 2:26-29). Having a circumcised heart by cutting away anything that should not be there is the requirement for all children of the King. Circumcising our hearts removes all that would interfere with intimacy, "that no human being might boast in the presence of God" (1 Cor. 1:29).

It interests me that Jesus found it so important to clear the temple; and even more so because unlike most incidences, it is recorded in all four Gospels (Matt. 21, Mark 11, Luke 19, John 2). The reason I find this slightly odd is that Jesus knew full well that, within a relatively short period of time, in the year 70 A.D., the temple would be destroyed and the sacrificial system would collapse. Clearing the temple would have a minimal, short-term impact. In a book that has limited space, why would we hear of this incident not once, but four times? What is the relevance to us as New Covenant believers?

Obviously, we do not want our modern churches to turn into "den[s] of thieves" (Matt. 21:13), places where the sheep are fleeced and not fed, places that neglect prayer and the essentials. But in light of 1 Corinthians 6:19-20, I believe there is another reason God felt it was so important that we know of Jesus clearing the temple. It reads, "Or do you not know that your body is a temple of the Holy Spirit within you, whom you have from God? You are not your own, for you were bought with a price. So glorify God in your body."

Our own temples (our selves) are to be places where communion with the Lord of heaven and earth can take place. Your very body is a "house of prayer"! I believe we need to routinely stand back and view our temples as Jesus would. Perhaps we need to start braiding a whip! We need to look objectively at what needs to be driven out. Have our priorities gotten out of whack? Have we sold out to the money changers until the only activity of our *Abba's* house is commerce?

I love our Lord's actions in this event. He is angry—violently angry. But His anger is not directed toward the genuine worshipper. His anger is at what is inhibiting their worship and their intimate relationship with the Father. That is what He is driving out—not the people but the barriers to the people and their connection to the God Who loves them. Likewise, when we ask Him to drive out what does not belong in our temples, He is loving enough to help us rid ourselves of any obstacle between us and the Father. What a loving God! What a gracious Lover to not want anything between us.

I want to continually rededicate myself to a cleared temple and renounce anything that would drive a wedge between my Lord and me. I declare that I am His temple, and I am a house of prayer! Lord, drive out the money changers, sweep the cobwebs from my heart, and come commune with me today, my Lord, my Love.

> *"Therefore, since we are surrounded by so great a cloud of witnesses, let us also lay aside every weight, and sin which clings so closely, and let us run with endurance the race that is set before us."*
>
> Heb. 12:1

DEVOTION

To be devoted implies a singularity of focus. Nothing is permitted to interfere with the object of your devotion. A deep devotion to the Lord will keep you from being easily thrown off course or discouraged in the process. A genuine hunger born out of an unwillingness to settle for mediocrity and flesh-comforting distance will be what energizes us when the road seems too steep to climb.

Have you ever noticed that all exclusive relationships can appear stifling from the outside perspective? It is only in the relationship—inside—where the love is felt and experienced, that the exclusivity transitions from stifling to safety, from confined to freedom. In a marriage, it is the exclusivity that speaks to the deepest love. It is the exclusivity that brings the greatest emotional freedom and security as it makes safe vulnerability possible.

Even in our walk with the Lord, we find this to be true. From the outside, it can look like merely stifling rules and regulations. It is only from inside this relationship all of that disappears and moves to the background, as we fall deeper and deeper in love. It is when we have come to a place of transitioning from acquaintances to inseparably intimate companions that exclusivity is welcomed as all we want in life. Where others may become offended by the words of the Lord and turn away, we cry out with Peter in an expression of devotion, "'Lord, to whom shall we go? You have the words of eternal life'" (John 6:68).

One of my personal favorite analogies in the Old Testament is in Exodus 21. The Lord is giving out laws on how to deal well with slaves and solve some of the predicaments that arise. He says, "'But if the servant declares, *I love my master . . . and do not want to go free*, then his master . . . shall take him to the door or the doorpost and pierce his ear with an awl. Then he will be his servant for life'" (vv. 5-6 NIV). This might sound kind of odd on the surface, but I find it a beautiful picture of that transitional decision to not just serve God because we must but to serve Him because we want nothing but Him.

Our hearts have been captured—not against our will, but captured by a love so complete that we simply cannot resist. We have experienced other loves—loves that left us empty and wanting, loves that promised to warm us but left us colder than when we came. We have experienced the selfish loves, the grasping loves, the domineering loves, the fading loves, the passive loves, or the distracted loves. We have experienced the imperfections of love, but every imperfection only served to point out that we cannot find what we are looking for in humans but only in God. This love we long for is available; our hearts know it must be so.

We were birthed out of the very heart of God's love. He conceived us and created us, and now our wandering hearts search to reconnect with that love and the One Who is Love. When we find Love and our hearts grow in trust, we then cry out, "I'm Yours!" We place our hearts in the hands of this Perfect Love. We allow the awl to pierce us, to mark us as His own. We choose the discomfort of growth over the illusion of safety that remaining in our shell would give. Every part of our broken selves we can trustingly surrender now.

The things of this world will never be able to satisfy us as our spirits yearn to be satisfied. The vacancy we feel within us, the constant longing and hunger for more, the knowledge that something is missing can only be fulfilled by this deep relationship with our Heavenly Father. Our spirits cannot thrive on what this world offers. The best we can hope for is meager subsistence. "Man does not live by bread alone, but man lives by every word that comes from the mouth of the LORD" (Deut. 8:3). And we hear those precious words from the mouth of the Lord from the place of companionship with Him.

God longs for those who are devoted to Him, who desire Him and His will more than their own lives. "Who is he who will devote himself to be close to me?" (Jer. 30:21 NIV). Are we willing to leave behind the distractions of this world and pursue our Lord? We cannot be devoted to the Lord and devoted to this world. We must choose where our allegiances lie. There is a direct correlation between our ability to get closer to God and our ability to not be distracted by the world. We lose our grip on God as we try to hold on to other things.

> *"And Mary said, 'Behold, I am the servant of the Lord;*
> *let it be to me according to your word.'"*
>
> Luke 1:38

PERSISTENCE

There is effort that is required, a pressing past the mob of people who are crowding the outer courts. Sometimes, our pursuit of intimacy with the Lord can even cause those around us such discomfort with their own lack of companionship with the Lord that they seek to block our way. This is not something new but can be seen throughout the Word of God. We see Moses pursuing the Lord and his own sister, Miriam, coming against him. We see David worshipping God with every fiber of his being and his wife, Michal, deriding him. We see Hannah in deep prayer and the high priest, Eli, who had lost his first Love, falsely accusing her of drunkenness. We see Mary pouring out the nard on the feet of Jesus, only to suffer the accusation of neglecting the poor by the disciples.

Over and over, we see that those who are true worshippers are misunderstood and reviled by those whose hearts are cold or jealous. They are stuck in their "religiosity"; and unless they relinquish the desire to be culturally appropriate to the desire to be in relationship, they will retire in their spiritual leprosy and barrenness.

We must press past them and press on to touch the Lord, as the woman with the issue of blood pressed through the crowd to touch the hem of Jesus' garment (Luke 8:43-48). We must not relent, though we be assaulted by the "watchmen of the walls" as the beloved was as she searched for the lover (Song of Songs 5:7). We must pursue all that the Lord has promised to us, though our own pharaohs intimidate us and try to tell us that we can only have so much worship and no more (Exod. 8:25, 28; 10:10, 24).

Let us not be those who give up just shy of the goal. Let us not put in effort only to waste it by walking away. This is the pearl of great price, and if we are willing to sell all for it, we may have it. Do not miss out because you place too little value on it. And never place a higher value on the opinion of man than on your relationship with your Abba.

But this goal we are pressing toward is not a destination. We cannot arrive and simply settle in. Like any good relationship, it is not enough to establish it; we must cultivate it. We must continue to press forward. The presence of God is addictive, but the world will not stop trying to throw its distractions at you. Persistence is called for to launch the relationship, and persistence is called for to keep it moving forward.

"For you have need of endurance, so that when you have done the will of God you may receive what is promised."

Heb. 10:36

HUMILITY

I live in a desert—a dry desert. When we say, "It's a dry heat," we mean that when you step outside, you can literally feel the moisture being sucked out of your body.

One of my daughters and I recently took a brief trip to the beautiful state of Tennessee, a foreign country to me. I'm not just referring to the accent, the speed of life, or the plethora of Christian radio stations. It is green—without manmade irrigation! Apparently, while you sleep at night, water comes out of the Tennessee air and condenses on the grass and flowers; and then it actually stays there all day, even in the sunshine!

There is another weird phenomenon. Wherever the ground is depressed, water gathers. I am not kidding—the whole area is dotted and crisscrossed by bodies of water. Where I live, the low places are extra dusty and give birth to dust devils. What an interesting concept to think of low places filling with water.

It made me think of my life and how I want to be filled with Jesus. However, He cannot fill something that is already full. I need to get lower—be less filled with myself. More of Him requires less of me. It is a natural cause and effect. The humbler I become, the more of Him I will be filled with just as water flows to the deepest areas. This is how the humble are exalted; this is the honor of humility (Matt. 23:12). The humble are exalted because they are full of God.

This task in life of coming to this humble place and rejoicing in it is so vital. We come there by means of our realization of the magnitude and majesty of God and our realization of our place as created beings. We are His creations and are meant to spend our lives honoring, serving, and communing with Him.

We cannot come to humility by self-deprecation, though that is our first instinctual attempt at humility. But the use of self-deprecation is merely an attempt to use a demonic device to conquer a demonic condition. The devil is the author of pride and the accuser of the brethren. We must reject his condition (pride) *and* his methods (accusation).

Instead, we must learn humility from the Author and best example of humility: the Lamb of God. We must attach ourselves to Him and match Him step for step (this is the essence of taking His yoke upon ourselves). We must learn from Him Who is "gentle and lowly in heart" (Matt. 11:29).

This reduction of self from the equation empowers us to every other glory. The glory of communion with God is birthed in the humble heart. Great service done in the Father's name is only effective with a humble spirit. It is a heart of humility that keeps itself in proper relationship to the Lord that can also keep itself in proper relationship with those around and be an accurate representative of the Lord.

> *"Humble yourselves before the Lord,*
> *and he will exalt you."*
>
> James 4:10

WISDOM AND REVELATION

Repeatedly, the Bible tells us to learn, study, and meditate on the words of the Lord. The acquisition of knowledge, words, and character of God is to be a daily business of every believer. Head knowledge is important. It is crucial to know the ways of the Lord by studying the Word, but we must also come to know God intimately and experientially, lest we become like the Pharisees to whom Jesus said, "'You search the Scriptures because you think that in them you have eternal life; and it is they that bear witness about me, yet you refuse to come to me that you may have life'" (John 5:39-40). They knew every jot and tittle of the Scriptures, yet they could not see God when He stood before them.

Knowledge is good, but knowledge alone puffs us up (1 Cor. 8:1). That is why Paul told the Ephesians that he continually prayed that God "may give [them] the Spirit of wisdom and of revelation in the knowledge of him" (1:17). It is by wisdom and revelation that we have intimate knowledge of God, not simply by studying about Him.

Wisdom is God-given. It is rightly applied knowledge. True wisdom will often not line up with the wisdom of our day. Unbelievers and even carnally minded believers will not comprehend when we endeavor to enter and abide in the Presence of the Lord. However, "the foolishness of God is wiser than men" (1 Cor. 1:25).

Revelation is also God-given and is completely independent from knowledge. Revelation gives you insight you could never have attained through learning. If we desire revelation, we are completely dependent on the graciousness of God giving it to us. Yet Jesus promises, *"All things have been handed over to me by my Father, and no one knows the Son except the Father, and no one knows the Father except the Son and anyone to whom the Son chooses to reveal him"* (Matt. 11:27).

Knowing God through wisdom and revelation can be frustrating as it requires utter dependence on the benevolence of God to give it to us. We cannot earn it or obtain it by our own means. Yet God promises that "if any of you lacks wisdom, let him ask God, who gives generously to all without reproach, and it will be given him" (James 1:5). Faith will remind us of the love that God has for us and remember "your Father who is in heaven give[s] good things to those who ask him!" (Matt. 7:11).

> *"Seek the LORD and his strength; seek his presence continually!"*
>
> Psalm 105:4

CHAPTER 15

TROUBLESHOOTING SILENCE

WHEN OUR OLDEST DAUGHTER WAS in junior high, I took a giant leap of faith and homeschooled her. Homeschooling is not for the faint of heart, as the 2020 pandemic taught many parents. But through the pre-algebra, American history, and biology, it was an amazing time of bonding and growth in our relationship.

Because we could see all the benefits of one-on-one time with her and in part to give me a moment, my husband would almost exclusively tuck her in at night and take some time to chat with her, growing their one-on-one relationship at bedtime as I had the opportunity to do throughout the day. Sometimes, he was up there for a few minutes; more often, I could hear their chatting and laughter stretch into thirty or more minutes (partly caused by our daughter's realization that the longer she talked, the later she could stay up). It was a blessing to their relationship, and I was so blessed to have married a man who could hold his own in a conversation with our loquacious girl.

Many do not grow up with the blessing of a father who is proficient at communication. Many have grown up with fathers too busy or exhausted, too stereotypically strong and silent, too caught up in their own lives to be present for us. It leaves us broken in one of the most central areas of our emotional and spiritual lives. It leaves us wondering if God sees us, hears us, and speaks to us.

Trying to hear from our Heavenly Father is not always a thing that comes easily or without real effort and practice to press in to feel that whisper stirring in our hearts. And it is in those times when we are just starting to press in that we can easily be put off by our apparent inability to hear.

There are other times when life seems to be collapsing at our feet or when an immediate decision is required, but it seems we have suddenly lost our connection to the still, small Voice that guides us so gently. Why does that Voice disappear at times?

We will all have times when it seems that no matter how hard we press in to try to hear what God is saying, we hear nothing but deafening silence.

Here are a few of the things I have learned about God during those times. (And is it not amazing that we can continue to learn so much from Him, even when He is silent? He is just that deep!)

1. "Trust Your Abba's Heart." We have already discussed how fear of rejection can limit our expectation of being able to hear when we first begin this journey. But that haunting fear that this Father is also too busy or too impersonal to speak to us tries to sneak its way back into our hearts, and the accuser comes with his attempts to make you feel like the odd one out. The resultant lack of faith and expectancy cuts us off like a switch has turned off our ears. It isn't that God is not speaking. It is that we have lost the necessary ingredient of hearing: faith in God's love and goodness (Heb. 11:6).

It is in these moments that we can simply restore our faith by speaking trusting words that affirm God's love and counteract the left-out-loser accusation. I will often say things like, "Thank You, Lord, for Your Presence right here with me. I thank You that You speak to me, that You want to speak even more than I want to hear. Thank You, Holy Spirit, for opening my ears to hear my Father's words."

2. "If I tell you, will you obey?" Can we be honest? Sometimes, deep down in our hearts, perhaps even undiscoverable without introspection and gut-exposing honesty, we have a certain thing we want to hear from the Lord in a given situation. If there are two options before me, there is often one that I particularly want the Lord to sanction, one I am trying to sell Him, one that I am sure will make me happier.

We may hear nothing when our minds are magnetized to our favorite option. It takes a willingness to hear either option that gives us the clarity to hear at all. Coming before the Lord and laying down our own will does wonders for opening our ears.

Know that if you get your way in something that is not God's will, it will not be a blessing in your life, no matter how much you think it will be. Heed the fearful warning the Lord gave through Ezekiel: "Say to those who prophesy from their own hearts . . . They say, 'Declares the LORD,' when the LORD has not sent them, and yet they expect him to fulfill their word . . . Therefore thus says the Lord GOD: 'Because you have uttered falsehood and seen lying visions, therefore behold, I am against you, declares the Lord GOD'" (13:2, 6, 8).

3. "What did I already tell you?" Similar to the previous one but different in motivation, sometimes I am just moving ahead of God. He has given me some directive, and I have meant to get to it but have not. Sometimes, I have noticed that His silence is telling me to finish what He has told me to do.

Having a chatterbox child taught me this. Sometimes, I would just stare at her blankly until she realized that in spite of the fact she continued to chatter, I was still waiting for her to do what I had told her to do. I can just picture the Lord with that same blank expression as I prattle on about everything and then wonder why He is just standing there silently. So patiently, He is waiting for me to get a clue. "Oh yeah! I was supposed to do what He already asked!"

I have always found it somewhat humorous that in the book of Jonah, God tells Jonah to go to Nineveh and remains silent until Jonah has been spewed from the fish. God does not say one more word to Jonah until He repeats the same instruction: "Go to Nineveh!" (paraphrased from Jonah 1:2

and 3:2). Sometimes, all it takes is a thumbing through my journal to realize I was given an instruction, and I need to follow through.

4. "Take baby steps." Incremental obedience is often the course God has for us. It is extremely unlikely that He will show us the whole map. He is much more likely to show us the end goal and just the one little step ahead of us to take. And when we have obeyed the little instruction in front of us, another is given.

Be willing to obey in the little things that seem like they will not make a difference. Obedience always makes a difference. There is a basic biblical principle at play here. When you are faithful with little, you will be entrusted with more (Matt. 25:14-30). Obedience opens you up to hearing more, obeying more, and receiving more. The reverse is also true—repeated disobedience callouses the heart and the ear. Continually brush aside the little instruction and guidance of the Lord, and you will hear less and less instruction and guidance.

5. "Who are you focused on?" The other day I had gotten a bit pensive, so my husband asked me what I was thinking about. The truth was I was on the verge of throwing myself a mini pity party. I already had my little hat on and was blowing up the balloons when he asked. I did not think he wanted to be on the invitation list, so I answered, singing a scale, "Me, me, me, me, ME, me, me, me, me!" Party over.

Sometimes when we pray, we need to just get a bigger view than "me and mine." God is, of course, concerned for every detail of our lives, but a sign of maturity is being able to see past the end of our own noses! God's silence can serve to snap us out of our egocentric thinking and remind us that it is not all about us.

6. "You're asking the wrong question." Even if we are looking in the right direction, we may be looking at the wrong thing. I can get so intent on one subject that it is all I want to ask Him about, like the disciples asking Jesus after the Resurrection, "Lord, will you at this time restore the kingdom to Israel?" (Acts 1:6). If I were Jesus, I would have just shaken my head and said, "You just don't get it, do you?"

Often, God has so much more for us than what our temporal eyes can see. When He is silent, not answering your questions, it pays to just sit back and ask Him what is on His mind! Reset your heart to beat in rhythm with His.

7. "Rekindle your passion." Of course, in any relationship, there will be times when passion may wax and wane. Humanity is subject to the ebb and flow of intense emotion. The key is to not pay the ebb too much heed. Checking your heart will let you know if there is too much of the world, your flesh, or something else that is hindering your intimacy.

If the Holy Spirit does not show you anything to deal with in your heart, know that the ebb is part of the package of relationship and spend time stoking the fires of passion for the Lord. Turn your gaze to the beauty of God's grace and love for you; worship and adore Him for His kindness, awe-stirring power, and saving mercy. As your eyes get filled with the wonder of the Lord, let weariness and apathy melt away. Remember we can have nothing that is not given us by the Father. Whatever you have need of, ask of Him and then trust Him with what comes. If you long for more desire, ask Him for more desire. Wherever you find a lack, He has a desire to fill. Ask Him to fill you as I did during this journal entry:

> *I have been feeling rejection because my time with the Lord has been falling far below my expectations. As we prayed, I felt the Lord reminding me of the story of the indebted woman who was instructed to fill every available vessel (2 Kings 4). As in Creation, God fills every available vessel. I need to trust the Lord will fill me as I am available. God's ability to fill is limited only by our availability. Where our availability stops, so does the filling and the anointing. Dear God, fill this vessel (April 2008).*

8. "What is stored in your heart?" When it comes to hearing from the Lord, some of us have not stored up enough of God's Word in our hearts to discern if it is our Father speaking or not. If "faith comes from hearing, and hearing through the word of Christ" (Rom. 10:17), being proficient in the written Word of God will enhance our ability to hear when He guides us through other means. Being a hearer and a doer of the written Word (James 1:22) makes us able to handle more of the spoken word of God. It is a safeguard we cannot bypass as we launch out into the deep that calls to deep.

9. "What filter is altering your hearing?" Knowing the Word of God not only helps us hear; that knowledge also helps us distinguish between God's voice and the voice of our flesh or the enemy. Because we often hear through a filter shaped by our parents, that mean kid at school, a teacher you could never please, or your own inner critic, our minds need to be renewed to what God says about us. We need to get to know His character to filter out things He would never say to us.

If we are hearing hopelessness and condemnation, that is not from our Abba Father. He will convict us of sin, but it will always be laced with hope and direction for a new path. If we are hearing God drive us or demean us like slaves, we need to remind ourselves that He treats us as beloved sons and daughters. If we think we hear God speaking condemnation or judgment over others, we need to remember that God's voice will not speak more unkindly about others than He does about us. Whatever we hear needs to measure up to what God has revealed about His will and His character within the written Word of God.

10. "I've got a plan." There are times I wrestle with God. I am sure I need the information I want right now. I need direction! What am I going to do? Which road do I take? Should I give up or keep going? Just tell me what to do! I remember one time, crying out to God like this, and He so clearly told me, "You don't need to know as much as you think you do." Wow. What I need to know is far less than what I want to know. I simply needed to embrace trusting rest. If I can check my heart and find it available and obedient, I can trust that I will receive the direction I need when I need it.

11. "This is a test of the Emergency Broadcasting System. This is only a test." Even in the natural, listening does not come naturally. It requires training. That is why the EBS runs those obnoxious tests on the radio and television. In listening for God's voice, there is so much growth that comes just by developing the maturity to sit and wait—even when nothing comes.

I cannot tell you how many times I have sat with my silent Abba, only to have Him drop a bomb of revelation in the last two minutes before I have to leave my house! God shows Himself faithful to those who are faithful (2 Sam. 22:26). And maturity must include maintaining faith in silence.

The question is whether you are willing to press in, though you hear nothing for days, weeks, months. Are you willing to say, "Lord even if You are silent, I will show myself faithful and trust You to speak in Your good timing"? There have been times in the past when I would listen with all I had and hear nothing. I would think, "Well, that was pointless." But I have learned that nothing done in an effort to grow closer to God is pointless. While I did not get what I had hoped for that day, I sowed seed that will continue to feed me the rest of my life.

Yes, God can be silent, but it is silence that speaks volumes! Words are not always necessary between lovers. But this is what true lovers do: they listen and hear, even when nothing is said.

> *"I wait for the LORD, my soul waits, and in his word I hope; my soul waits for the Lord more than watchmen for the morning, more than watchmen for the morning."*
>
> Psalm 130:5-6

CHAPTER 16
WELCOMING AND ABIDING IN THE PRESENCE

LIFE CAN BE BUSY—OUTRAGEOUSLY BUSY. When my husband and I were raising our littles, we were advised to develop the habit of daily time together, just the two of us, at the outset of our evenings. We just needed ten to fifteen minutes to reconnect at the end of the workday—before dinner, homework help, and bedtime rituals with our kids began. It was a brilliant idea and helped to keep us connected and as close to "on the same page" as two parents can get.

Often, our evening meetings went longer than the allotted time; but more times than not, there was no time during our initial conversation to move past the catching up of the day and the to-do list. We did not take the time to push past the "head-to-head" conversation to the two hearts communicating—the loving and flirting and intimate heart-sharing.

And often, our times with the Lord can default to the same "head conversation." There is nothing in the world wrong with our questions that seek the Lord's wisdom, letting Him show us solutions for our day-to-day needs, letting Him show us what needs to be done and what the truth is about the battles we are facing. All of that is such an incredible blessing! To know that the God Who created the universe loves us so much that He helps us with our—in the scheme of things—piddly problems and questions, brings us a joy of knowing that He cares for the tiniest details in our lives.

Yet what about moving beyond the head conversation to the two hearts communicating? It is one thing to know we are partnering with God in our journey, to see the Kingdom come in our life, our families' lives, and our community. But deeper than partnering, we are also called to be lovers of the Lord, to enjoy His Presence, and to rejoice as He sings over us with dancing.

Our pastor shared with us this simple prayer that helps me to move past the task-oriented prayers that can be so easy to gravitate toward: "Lord, would You just come and love on me right now?" What a powerful prayer! To rest from the busyness that consumes not only our time, but also our minds, and to bask—simply bask—in our identity as lovers of God.

Your Abba rejoices over you, Dear Friend. He wants you to enjoy His enjoyment of you, to marvel in His loving friendship, and to know that He knows you and loves you without measure. There is Someone Who wants to spend time with you, to laugh and chat and share with you. He never gets tired of you, bored by you, or annoyed by you. Let Him enjoy you.

> *"The LORD your God is in your midst, a mighty one who will save;*
> *he will rejoice over you with gladness; he will quiet you by his love;*
> *he will exult over you with loud singing."*
>
> Zeph. 3:17

MAINTAIN AWE

We can be companions with God. What an incredible invitation the Lord extends to us—His children and His creations. Yet companionship does not make us equal with God.

All this access, this companionship, has to be seen in the light of God's overpowering majesty. In truth, we can only truly appreciate the access when we have the realization of exactly Who we are granted access to! Only a sense of awe is appropriate when we consider His great splendor. The King of the universe, the Creator of all, wants to be our Friend.

When we stand apart and distant, it offends God's generous heart. Conversely, losing our sense of awe offends His generosity equally because we have lost sight of how amazing His gift is and how far He has stooped to make us great.

It was over-familiarity that cost Uzzah his life. The story of Uzzah comes from 2 Samuel 6. The ark had been in the house of Uzzah's father for around twenty years. He had become so familiar with it as all of life went on, day in and day out, with the ark in his home. No doubt, it was an honored piece of furniture—but a piece of the furniture, nonetheless. That familiarity put Uzzah in a precarious position when the day came to move the ark to Jerusalem. As the cart carrying the ark hits the bump in the road, Uzzah reaches out to steady the ark, a fatal mistake.

The Philistines had repeatedly had to stand their idol, Dagon, back up when it fell (1 Sam. 5:1-4), but *Yahweh* needed no such help.

So, is *Yahweh* a distant, far-off God, unapproachable and happy to stay at arm's length? Or is He your Buddy, content to be treated as a piece of the furniture? Neither!

He is most definitely approachable, most definitely kind, and desiring to be our Friend. And yet, I want to encourage you to ponder—really meditate on the beautiful reality—that He is God, our King, before whom all the elders of heaven bow, crying out, "Holy!" It is this great God that has called you near, yes, to run into His arms and be embraced. Feel the awe of this today and marvel at His great love for you. The holiness of God does not detract from the sweetness of His nearness; instead, it makes His desire for nearness all the sweeter.

> *"You have given me the shield of your salvation, and your right hand supported me, and your gentleness made me great."*
>
> Psalm 18:35

THE BEAUTY OF ABIDING

When we have experienced the manifest Presence of God, once is not enough. The place of companionship is our home; it is the place of experiencing the Presence of God—the Presence that we were created to dwell in at all times. But how exactly can we live in two places at once? How can we cope in the work-a-day world and still maintain connection to God? This is where abiding comes in.

Following a windy day several years ago, our then three-and-a-half-year-old grandson was playing in our backyard with my husband. I came outside to see how things were going, and my grandson proudly showed me a collection of about twenty underdeveloped oranges he had collected from the ground beneath the wind-blown orange tree and placed in a small dish. The poor oranges ranged in color from yellow to black and from the size of peas to marbles. Cheerfully, he exclaimed, "See all my oranges, Grandmama?" Then, with all the excitement he could express, he announced, "Someday, they're gonna be *big* oranges!"

I pointed to the green oranges that remained on the tree, saying, "These oranges up here will get really big, Buddy. But those oranges"—pointing to the dish—"won't get any bigger."

"Why not?" he asked sorrowfully.

"Because, Bud, those oranges aren't connected to the tree anymore. The oranges have to stay connected to the tree in order to grow big."

Those poor, pathetic oranges were still oranges; they were still round; and some were even turning yellow like oranges always do before they turn orange. They could appear to be normal. But something went wrong. They were no longer connected.

It reminds me of one of the saddest verses in Scripture (in my opinion, anyway). It occurs when Delilah has cut off Samson's hair and he does not know it yet. She wakes him by yelling, "The Philistines are upon you, Samson!"

He thinks, *No problem! I'll go defeat them as I have before*. Then, the Scripture tells us, "But he did not know that the LORD had left him" (Judges 16:20).

So sad. He is clueless—and helpless! He has taken the anointing hand of the Lord so much for granted that he cannot even tell when it has been lifted from him. How often we go through life thinking we've got it together and not realizing that because we have let go of Abba's hand, we are wandering, about to be blinded because we thought we could wing it on our own.

Abiding is the key. Jesus says in John 15:4, "'Abide in me, and I in you. As the branch cannot bear fruit by itself, unless it abides in the vine, neither can you, unless you abide in me.'" Unless we are abiding in the Vine, there is no chance we are going to bear any fruit. But what exactly does it mean to "abide"? I always thought it meant to stay close, but if we consider a literal vine, it takes on a deeper meaning.

In a vineyard, all the branches of a vine grow directly from the primary stock. A branch cannot piggyback off another branch; it must be connected only to the true vine. So, it is with us and our Lord.

Each year, the branches in a vineyard are cut back until they are only about an inch long. For nearly a year, they "abide" in the vine, and the vine expands and grows all around the little nub of a branch. Suddenly, after soaking up all the nutrients of the vine, the branches grow out quickly and are able to produce fruit.

I'm looking for that place where I can crawl inside and abide within the Vine—that place where I can hide away in my Shelter and soak Him up, where all of me is pruned away except for the part that is one with Him. Then I'll be abiding, and then I'll be growing.

> *"I am the vine; you are the branches. Whoever abides in me and I in him, he it is that bears much fruit, for apart from me you can do nothing."*
>
> John 15:5

Brother Lawrence described his experience of abiding like this:

> I began to live as if there was none but He and I in the world . . . I worshipped Him the oftenest that I could, keeping my mind in His holy presence, and recalling it as often as I found it wandered from Him . . . without troubling or disquieting myself when my mind had wandered involuntarily. I made this my business as much all the day long as at the appointed times of prayer; for at all times, every hour, every minute, even in the height of my business, I drove away from my mind everything that was capable of interrupting my thought of God.[14]

This practice of living in the presence of God is abiding—focusing on Him at all times and dwelling inwardly with the Lord regardless of what is going on outwardly. Brother Lawrence, working away in the kitchen of a monastery, with all its noise, busyness, and demanding responsibilities, did not have it easy when it came to abiding. His life was every bit as distracting as ours can be. Yet he found a way to make it work. He trained his mind to continually be drawn to the Presence of God. He did not chide himself when his mind wandered (as he wisely said, deriding ourselves would only make our minds wander further and longer), but he simply led his mind back to God as often as it took.

Though our minds may flood us with doubts about the impossibility of remaining in the presence of God, through faith, we will see it come to pass that as we continue in the habit, it becomes our second nature, as undeniable as the need to breathe. But it is only for those who will press on and say with the psalmist, "One thing have I asked of the LORD, that will I seek after: that I may dwell in the house of the LORD all the days of my life, to gaze upon the beauty of the LORD and to inquire in his temple" (Psalm 27:4).

This is the intimate relationship that we are to desire. This is the place of sweet companionship that God longs for you to have with Him. It is the

---

14 Brother Lawrence, *The Practice of the Presence of God* (Westwood: Fleming H. Revell, 1958), 33.

place of belonging. It is not a place reserved for a few elite Christians, but it is the place all believers are called to by the wooing of the Holy Spirit. It will require a heart that is hungry and persistent—a believing, repentant heart. It will not be a quick and easy process, but it is well worth any effort.

"Let all our employment be to *know* God; the more one knows Him, the more one desires to know Him. And as knowledge is commonly the measure of love, the deeper and more extensive our knowledge shall be, the greater will be our love."[15]

"Let us know; let us press on to know the LORD; his going out is sure as the dawn; he will come to us as the showers, as the spring rains that water the earth."

Hosea 6:3

Journal reflection on Psalm 84:

PSALM 84

(The Valley of Baca)[16]

A pilgrimage—a road less traveled—
To Your heart I long to go.
Seems to be a life unraveled;
Your inner court I yearn to know.
Strength to strength, You lead me on
Till all the pain I feel is gone.

A valley of tears lies between us—
Between the present and the call.

---

15 Ibid., 63.
16 Baca means, "weeping."

CONSTANT COMPANION

A fire in me won't let me give up.
Lord, You know I want it all.
The salty flood I pour out to You
Is greeted by Your autumn rains.
Pools of blessing lead me on
To this Your dwelling place.

A heart so low, it can't look up.
A pain so deep, it can't be ignored.
Jesus come and fill the cup.
A splash of tears—the first to pour.
Leaving wells for one behind me,
Despite the hurting, they'll know You and see.

Make me a sparrow, so I can be
In Your courts always to sing.
Better the life span of a songbird
With just a moment at Your side
Than to live forever but without You
And never know You as my Guide.

(May 2002)

BIBLIOGRAPHY

Lawrence, Brother. *The Practice of the Presence of God.* Westwood, New Jersey: Fleming H. Revell, 1958.

Lewis, C.S. *Lion, the Witch and the Wardrobe, The.* New York, New York: Collier, 1976.

Lewis, C.S. *Mere Christianity.* Westwood, New Jersey: Barbour and Company, Inc., 1943.

Rees, Wilbur. *$3.00 Worth of God.* Valley Forge, Pennsylvania: Judson Press, 1971.

Strong, James. *New Strong's Exhaustive Concordance.* Nashville, Tennessee: Thomas Nelson Publishers, 1996.

Tanakh: A New Traditional Hebrew Text and the New JPS Translation. Philadelphia, Pennsylvania: Jewish Publication Society, 2003.

Vine, W.E. *Vine's Complete Expository Dictionary of the Old and New Testament Words.* Nashville, Tennessee: Thomas Nelson, Inc.,1996.

ABOUT THE AUTHOR

AMI HAS BEEN PREACHING SINCE her teens and has her master's degree in theology. A gleeful puzzler, a persistent solution-finder, and a hunter of clarity, Ami finds her joy in discovering connections and truths tucked in corners of the Word of God. As an author and guest speaker in churches and at conferences, she brings those truths to light as she crafts words that bring transformation. Ami's mission is to use the challenges she's been through to provide resources for others to propel them toward freedom by offering hope to the wounded, spiritual nourishment to the hungry, tools to the learners, and companionship to those who feel invisible.

Ami and her husband live in Arizona, and they love few things more than surrounding themselves with their children and their growing number of grandchildren.

Connect with Ami on her website, amiloper.com, and on social media, where you can find her by name.

Ambassador International's mission is to magnify the Lord Jesus Christ and promote His Gospel through the written word.

We believe through the publication of Christian literature, Jesus Christ and His Word will be exalted, believers will be strengthened in their walk with Him, and the lost will be directed to Jesus Christ as the only way of salvation.

For more information about
AMBASSADOR INTERNATIONAL
please visit:

www.ambassador-international.com
@AmbassadorIntl
www.facebook.com/AmbassadorIntl

Thank you for reading this book!

You make it possible for us to fulfill our mission, and we are grateful for your partnership.

To help further our mission, please consider leaving us a review on your social media, favorite retailer's website, Goodreads or Bookbub, or our website.

MORE FROM AMBASSADOR INTERNATIONAL

Finding Hope and Strength in God is a twelve-month devotional with different themes for each month focused on pointing you to your all-sufficient Savior, Who will give you strength and hope to face the day and to live a meaningful and fulfilling Christian life. Its practical approach to life will help you navigate real-life situations with tangible solutions to help you find meaning, hope, strength, and courage despite the tumultuous eventualities of life.

God calls us all to live a life of purpose—to live prepared to be on mission and go where He needs us both locally and globally. Through life-shaping stories, *Unseen People* offers encouragement, inspiration and prepares our hearts when it's time to go. Sometimes the hard places He guides us to are next door, not around the world. The call is the same—to see and serve people, to hear and share their stories. You will be different. Their stories will shape you, change you and challenge you to keep going.

For many men, work, relationships, and life in general overwhelm their schedules and keep them from spending time with God. But what they don't realize is that joy is found in those moments spent with their Creator. In *Finding Joy in Every Season*, Chris Corradino provides brief devotionals for every day to help men get in the Word and start their day off right. Spending just ten minutes with God will realign your focus and help you find the joy that comes in the everyday moments.

www.ingramcontent.com/pod-product-compliance
Lightning Source LLC
Chambersburg PA
CBHW062222080426
42734CB00010B/1993